MIDDLEMARCH BY GEORGE ELIOT

MACMILLAN MASTER GUIDES

General Editor: James Gibson

Also published by Macmillan

MACMILLAN MASTER SERIES

Mastering English Literature R. Gill
Mastering English Language S. H. Burton
Mastering English Grammar S. H. Burton

MACMILLAN MASTER GUIDES

MIDDLEMARCH BY

GEORGE ELIOT

GRAHAM HANDLEY

MACMILLAN

First edition 1985

Published by
MACMILLAN EDUCATION LTD
Houndmills, Basingstoke, Hampshire RG21 2XS
and London
Companies and representatives
throughout the world

Printed in Hong Kong

British Library Cataloguing in Publication Data
Handley, Graham
Middlemarch by George Eliot.
1. Eliot, George. Middlemarch
I. Title
823'.8   PR4662
ISBN 0-333-39001-6 Pbk
ISBN 0-333-39688-X Pbk export

CONTENTS

To Barbara Hardy
with love

GENERAL EDITOR'S PREFACE

The aim of the Macmillan Master Guides is to help you to appreciate the book you are studying by providing information about it and by suggesting ways of reading and thinking about it which will lead to a fuller understanding. The section on the writer's life and background has been designed to illustrate those aspects of the writer's life which have influenced the work, and to place it in its personal and literary context. The summaries and critical commentary are of special importance in that each brief summary of the action is followed by an examination of the significant critical points. The space which might have been given to repetitive explanatory notes has been devoted to a detailed analysis of the kind of passage which might confront you in an examination. Literary criticism is concerned with both the broader aspects of the work being studied and with its detail. The ideas which meet us in reading a great work of literature, and their relevance to us today, are an essential part of our study, and our Guides look at the thought of their subject in some detail. But just as essential is the craft with which the writer has constructed his work of art, and this is considered under several technical headings – characterisation, language, style and stagecraft.

The authors of these Guides are all teachers and writers of wide experience, and they have chosen to write about books they admire and know well in the belief that they can communicate their admiration to you. But you yourself must read and know intimately the book you are studying. No one can do that for you. You should see this book as a lamppost. Use it to shed light, not to lean against. If you know your text and know what it is saying about life, and how it says it, then you will enjoy it, and there is no better way of passing an examination in literature.

JAMES GIBSON

ACKNOWLEDGEMENT

Cover illustration: *Coventry* by J. M. W. Turner. Courtesy of the Trustees of the British Museum.

1 GEORGE ELIOT

1.1 LIFE

Mary Ann Evans (later to adopt the pseudonym of 'George Eliot') was born at Arbury Farm, near Nuneaton, in 1819. She was the second daughter of Robert Evans, who managed the estates of the nearby prosperous Newdigate family. Mary Ann worshipped her father and idolised her brother Isaac (born 1816); she soon proved to be a child of precocious intellect, with a particular aptitude for languages and music, but her formative years saw the influence of her first teacher direct her into a narrow and somewhat sententious Evangelicalism. This yielded to a wider and more tolerant attitude after she had become friends with the free-thinking Charles Bray, his wife Cara and the latter's sister, Sara Hennell. Bray was a radical, interested in phrenology (the science which studies the faculties by the size and shape of the skull), while his brother-in-law, Charles Hennell, wrote a book which was to greatly influence Mary Ann's cast of thought and faith, *An Inquiry Concerning the Origin of Christianity* (1838), in which he voiced his doubts of the biblical accounts of miracles and saw the life of Jesus as historically based.

Mary Ann's faith was shaken, her quick and inquiring mind stirred to question and examine, and by 1842 she was in a crisis of doubt. She gave up going to church, being temporarily estranged from her father as a result, though she soon compromised in order to spare him further pain. Through the Brays she met Rufa Brabant, who was translating David Friedrich Strauss's *Life of Jesus*, a radical, critical examination of the gospels. When Rufa, now married to Charles Hennell, gave up the work, Mary Ann took it over, completing it in 1846.

After her father's death in 1849 she moved to London, where she lodged with the publisher John Chapman and his wife. Intent on independence, she found Chapman a fascinating man and, although she left the house because of his wife's (and mistress's) jealousy, he was able to promote her journalistic career. In 1851 he acquired the radical journal the *Westminster Review*, and Marian (as she now called herself) became his assistant editor. As a result she met most of the great radicals and free-thinkers of her time, probably fell in love with the philosopher Herbert Spencer in 1852, and met George Henry Lewes (1817-78) in the same year. This meeting was to change the course of her life. Lewes was a contributor to the *Review*, was widely cultured, having a reputation as critic, novelist, scientist and philosopher. He was the biographer of the great German writer Goethe (1749-1832); he was also unhappily married, but could not obtain a divorce because he had condoned his wife's adultery with their friend, Thornton Leigh Hunt.

Lewes and Marian fell in love and lived together from 1854 until his death in 1878. After a working honeymoon spent in Weimar, they returned to London, suffering some social ostracism because of their decision to set up home together. For Marian the rupture with her brother Isaac was to be permanent; he did not approve of her loss of faith or of her living with Lewes. Marian was later to sublimate the anguish of this in *The Mill on the Floss* (1860), where brother and sister drown together, their epitaph the poignant 'In their death they were not divided'. Meanwhile Lewes continued to work away at his philosophy and science, Marian at her articles and reviews until, in 1856, stimulated by Lewes's faith in her, Marian began to write fiction. Lewes sent the first story as from 'my clerical friend' to John Blackwood, the publisher of *Blackwood's Magazine*. Two more tales followed, the three being issued as *Scenes of Clerical Life*. They were an immediate success; Marian adopted the pseudonym of 'George Eliot' (George because it was Lewes's name) and became a celebrated writer overnight. She was acclaimed by Dickens, among others, who was astute enough to spot the woman's hand in her early fiction. From then on her life was one of continuing success both in the literary and social sense. She knew the great writers and thinkers of her time and won their respect and admiration; her strong moral views as expressed in her fiction ensured her acceptance in society. The woman who was openly living in what was regarded as sin became the moral lawgiver of her time, held her afternoon gatherings for the great, and came to be thought of as something of a seer.

In essence her religion was a religion of humanity; sceptical of dogma yet loving tradition and roots, she set a high premium on man's duty to man. And at her elbow throughout the twenty years of her fame was George Henry Lewes; he protected her from criticism (and particularly from adverse reviews of her novels), managed negotiations with her publishers, devoted himself to her every need and encouraged her to write on, giving her the praise and sympathy she needed. When he died in 1878 she was heartbroken but, eighteen months later, she married John Walter Cross, a banker twenty years her junior who had been a good friend both to her and to Lewes. They honeymooned in Venice, but she died six months later, in December 1880. Five years afterwards Cross published *George Eliot's Life as Related in her Letters*. His discretion and unscrupulous cutting preserved the image, but William Ewart Gladstone, the statesman, with ironic wit, described the book as 'a reticence in three volumes'.

1.2 WORKS

Strictly speaking, George Eliot's first work grew out of her scepticism, or perhaps was the result of it. She spent some years studying German biblical criticism and, as we have seen, had translated Strauss's *Life of Jesus* (1846) though her name does not appear on the title-page. This was an influential book which held that the supernatural aspects of Christianity were myth. Her next work was also a translation, of the German philosopher Ludwig Feuerbach's *Essence of Christianity* (1854). She could say of Feuerbach's religion of humanity 'I everywhere agree', for his main thesis is that the true God is to be found in 'the divinity of human nature'. Many years later George Eliot was to write that 'the idea of God, so far as it has been a high spiritual influence, is the ideal of a goodness entirely human (i.e. an exaltation of the human)'. Both these translations carry the weight and authority of a great intellect which, once it was allied to a creative impulse, was to provide her fiction with moral, philosophical, spiritual and humanitarian perspective as well as warmth and immediacy of feeling.

We should not ignore, however, her apprentice years of journalism, for she brought the discipline and judgement which are so much part of her own writing to bear on the work of others. Moreover, in an article like 'Silly Novels by Lady Novelists' she establishes, after a swingeing attack on the writers of this 'elegant boudoirs' school, what was to become central to her own fictional practice. Not only are diligence, responsibility and 'an appreciation of the writer's art' required, but also 'genuine observation, humour and passion'. These, as Bel Mooney, journalist and author, has rightly pointed out, are all 'directed towards one end, which I suppose we might call *sympathetic truth*'. It is the right phrase, indicating the compassion and warmth, altruism and perspective, which are at the core of George Eliot's art.

Scenes of Clerical Life (1857) reflects that love and concern for the past which informs her work throughout. The first of the *Scenes*, 'The Sad Fortunes of the Reverend Amos Barton', is notable for its evocation of that past in a small community, for its humour and its pathos, though the death-bed scene of Milly Barton has a heavy overlay of sentiment, almost Dickensian in its inescapable tearfulness. In 'Mr Gilfil's Love-story' George Eliot employs what was to become one of her favourite techniques, the use of retrospect, to describe the sad life of Maynard Gilfil and how his long loneliness came about. The third *Scene*, 'Janet's Repentance', is a masterpiece, foreshadowing in its psychological intensity and sympathetic insights the great novels to come. Janet, alcoholic wife of the brutal and domineering lawyer Dempster, is reclaimed by the practical Christian goodness of the Evangelical Edgar Tryan to a life of endeavour and dedication on behalf of others. This theme, of humanitarian or altruistic action, is to be sounded again and again.

In *Adam Bede* (1859) George Eliot fused the recollections of her

Warwickshire childhood with a story told her by her Methodist aunt, Elizabeth Evans, of a girl tried for child-murder. The period is that of the Napoleonic Wars (1793-1815), the novel's chronology spanning 1799-1807, but the subject as always is the interaction of people. The central characters are Adam himself (the good workman, though a little 'lifted up and peppery like'), Arthur Donnithorne, the well-meaning but egoistic and weak young squire, and Hetty Sorrel, the girl who is engaged to Adam and who is seduced by Arthur, misguidedly feeling that the young squire intends to marry her. This tragic tale is salted, as George Eliot's early work often is, with a rare rustic humour. This is seen directly in the character of Mrs Poyser, Hetty's aunt, whose dialect sharpness is both acidic and proverbial.

The Mill on the Floss (1860), though its location is Gainsborough (St Ogg's), is largely autobiographical, Tom and Maggie Tulliver approximating to Isaac and Mary Ann Evans. Maggie is one of the most sympathetically delineated of George Eliot's heroines, while the family tragedy of the Tullivers is poignantly felt by the reader. The running humour in the presentation of the idiosyncratic Dodson aunts – and particularly that of Mrs Glegg – acts as commentary on and evaluation of the main action. The ending, which sees Tom and Maggie, clasped in each other's arms, drown in the Floss, is a fictional expression of wish-fulfilment, the reconciliation in life with her own brother which George Eliot was denied.

She began research on her Italian novel *Romola* (1863), but turned away from it to write *Silas Marner* (1861), moved by the 'millet-seed' of thought by which she 'intended to set in a strong light the remedial influences of pure, natural human relations.' Silas himself – middle-aged, suffering from loss of faith and periodic catalepsy (fits of a trance-like nature) – is an unlikely hero, but this small novel exists on the levels of realism and fable, a kind of prose poem which exemplifies the Wordsworthian love of common humanity seen in the motto printed on the title-page of the first edition:

> A child, more than all others gifts
> That earth can offer to declining man,
> Brings hope with it, and forward-looking thoughts.

Romola is an historical novel full of strained idiom and researched rather than felt local colour, but it remains an enduring achievement. The focus, as ever, is really on personal relationships, and in the portrait of the weak, sensual egoist Tito and, even more strongly, in the obsessional and pathetic Baldassarre, his adoptive father, George Eliot achieved an integrated psychological consistency which makes their characters recognisably real despite the self-conscious 'placing' in distant time.

Her next novel was *Felix Holt the Radical* (1866), set at the time of the first great Reform Bill (1832). It is an uneven novel, Felix being rather too large for life and suffering too much from his author's tacit approval of his verbal and moral stances as well as his physical presence. But it contains another portrait of unerring psychological truth in the person of the suffering sinner Mrs Transome, whose past affair with the lawyer Jermyn brings that unscrupulous manipulator into direct conflict with their son. The latter's radical opportunism is stifled when he comes to know who his real father is.

Before she wrote her greatest novel, *Middlemarch* (1871-2) George Eliot produced a long poem, *The Spanish Gypsy* (1868), which has some thematic interest but little poetic merit. *Middlemarch* and her final novel, *Daniel Deronda*, were published in Books or Parts, the eight monthly instalments of *Daniel Deronda* appearing from February to September 1876. The novel moves towards Judaism through the central character, who, having been brought up as an English gentleman, finds out that he is a Jew, and determines to devote his life to the service of his people. This is an extension of the altruistic idealism found throughout the novels, but it has to be allowed that the Jewish sections of the novel are somewhat cloying. There is rich compensation in the English section, in which a girl at once ambitious, egoistic and neurotic, living in straitened circumstances which allow her little scope, eventually marries a man whose own egoism and compulsive will are stronger than hers. She marries him despite the moral recognition that it is wrong to do so, for he has a mistress and four children. Gwendolen Harleth is one of the most complete characters in English fiction; 'And see how the girl is known, inside out, how thoroughly she is felt and understood. . . . It is so deep, so true, so complete, it holds such a wealth of psychological detail, it is more than masterly', says Constantius in Henry James's *Daniel Deronda: a Conversation* (1876). There can be no higher praise. In 1880 George Eliot published *The Essays of Theophrastus Such*, which are rather sententious and not a little boring. Effectively, *Daniel Deronda* was her last great contribution to English fiction.

1.3 ACHIEVEMENT

George Eliot brought to her writing a wide and informed learning, a knowledge in depth of science, philosophy, religion, languages and their literatures, as well as a strong sense of moral and social responsibility. She painted the nature of her childhood impressions in unforgettable and arresting colours in her early novels, giving them historical perspective and authenticity, and peopling them with a spectrum of society from country rustic to country gentleman. The measure of her greatness is seen in an increasing intellectual expression of the form in which she had chosen to write. Her novels show an awareness of artistic organisation, a belief that the completeness of real life could best be captured by a like completeness of form in the novel, and a sense of structural coherence, what Henry

James was to call 'total relevance'. Like her great contemporaries, Dickens and Thackeray, like Jane Austen before her and Hardy, who followed her, she raised the status of the novelist's art from the respectable to the respected, from the romantic to the artistic, from the sentimental to the aesthetically and intellectually rigorous.

It is easy to see why George Eliot has been considered the first of the modern novelists. The investigation and exposure of a character's consciousness did not begin with James Joyce or Virginia Woolf, for such examinations are present in George Eliot's fiction from the very beginning, and always with that truth to human nature, with its frailties and changes, which makes great literature live for us. Frederick Myers, her admirer and contemporary, has written of how once she took as her text the three words God, Immortality, Duty, saying 'how inconceivable was the first, how unbelievable the second, and yet how peremptory and absolute was the third'. There is no more complete comment on the moral values which characterise her fiction and which she commends to her readers; perhaps it is that through her novels she released those feelings of guilt and insecurity which were so much a part of her own uncertain nature.

She brought to the English novel a high sense of dignity and moral purpose, of truth to life, of artistic integrity and dedication, of love and kindness and humanity, of practical living for others, of suffering which makes for compassion. The psychological immediacy of her presentations brings the reader into intimacy with character. The novelists of the twentieth century went to school to George Eliot, however critical they were of her mannerisms of style, or tone, or of the duty-cum-work ethic which she advocated. Her intellect was complemented by her humanity, her wisdom by a breadth of tolerance and understanding. No writer has seen more clearly into the nature of human relationships or revealed the vicissitudes of these individual lives more sympathetically. Her work is informed with love and exalted by artistic and moral integrity.

1.4 WRITING AND PUBLICATION OF *MIDDLEMARCH*

Middlemarch represents the fusion of two originally separate stories, the Featherstone, Vincy, Lydgate plot on the one hand and the Dorothea/Casaubon plot on the other. Jerome Beaty (see Further Reading), in his superb study of the manuscript of the novel (*Middlemarch from Notebook to Novel*, 1960), has suggested that the early Featherstone, Vincy and Lydgate parts of the book were written by 2 August 1869, but it was not until over a year later that George Eliot began a story called 'Miss Brooke' (November 1870). This she soon integrated with the other part, obviously changing the order in the process. By the end of December 1870 about 100 pages had been written, and by March 1871 a total of 236.

Lewes, as always, now assumed his role of George Eliot's business manager. In April 1871 he wrote that 'Mrs Lewes sees her way to finishing her new novel by this autumn', while by May he had virtually worked out the mode of publication. Since the novel would be longer than the customary three volumes, he proposed that it be published 'in *half-volume parts* either at intervals of one, or as I think better, two months' (*Letters* v, 145–6). As far back as 1836 the manner of serial publication had been set by Dickens's *Pickwick Papers*, which came out in 19 monthly parts, effectively 20, since the last one was a double number. Lewes was changing the format slightly and, in so doing, underlining the sense of structure of George Eliot's work in the part and in the whole – 'Each part would have a certain unity and completeness in itself with appropriate title.'

John Blackwood accepted the idea. George Eliot's publisher was both supportive friend and encouraging critic to her as he read her manuscripts. By June 1871 he was commenting on 'the old twaddler Brooke' and expressing his anxiety for Dorothea. He particularly liked the characterisation in Part 2, writing to George Eliot in July that 'all is so fresh and true to life. Each group that you introduce is a little book or study in itself.' (*Letters* v, 168.) She replied a few days later that she hoped 'there is nothing that will be seen to be irrelevant to my design, which is to show the gradual action of ordinary causes rather than exceptional' (*Letters* v, 168). It was agreed that the first part should be published in December 1871, and in August George Eliot read Lewes Part 3, then called 'Dorothea Married', later changed to 'Waiting for Death', a much more strongly unifying title. Blackwood expressed some doubts about Casaubon's letter of proposal, considering that Dorothea, even Dorothea, would see through it.

Middlemarch was issued as Lewes had planned, except that the bi-monthly idea was retained for the first six parts or books (December 1871–October 1872), but the last two were brought out in the following months of November and December 1872. As usual with George Eliot, she was writing on as the novel was being issued, finishing Book IV as Book II was published. The Finale was finished on 2 October 1872, and a month later George Eliot wrote to Alexander Main:

> When a subject has begun to grow in me I suffer terribly until it has wrought itself out – become a complete organism; and then it seems to take wing and go away from me. That thing is not to be done again – that life has been lived. (*Letters* v, 324)

Now it was not only John Blackwood who could praise, for *The Times* said that it was 'almost profane to speak of ordinary novels in the same breath with George Eliot's', while in March 1873, three months after the book's completion in parts, the reviewer said that 'There are few novels which will repay reading over again so well as *Middlemarch*.' It was virtually three years in the writing; by 1879, the year before George Eliot died, it had sold nearly 34 000 copies, George Eliot's literary earnings from its sale being in the region of £9000, in modern money some quarter of a million pounds.

2 SUMMARIES
AND
CRITICAL COMMENTARY

In this section all chapters have individual commentaries, preceded by a summary of each Book.

PRELUDE

Summary

This contains a brief account of the life of St Theresa of Avila (1515-82), the Spanish nun and mystic who reformed the Carmelite order. Although Blackwood's London manager, Joseph Munt Langford, wrote to his employer 'I do not like the "Prelude" . . . I would omit it' there is every reason for its inclusion since it underpins George Eliot's sense of total relevance.

Commentary

The style is elevated as befits a subject of spiritual and idealistic exaltation like St Theresa, but the emphasis looks forward to all those failed St Theresas, each of whom is, supposedly, a 'foundress of nothing'. The implication is that we are to follow the life of one of these, and the rhetorical repetition of 'Here and there' is itself the prelude to an analogy with nature and prophetic of the history of Dorothea (and, by association, of Lydgate).

BOOK I   MISS BROOKE

Summary

The novel opens with a description of Dorothea Brooke, her sister Celia and their uncle Mr Brooke. This is followed by a dinner party given by Mr Brooke, his guests being a neighbouring baronet, Sir James Chettam, and Mr Casaubon, clergyman and scholar. The latter conveys how lonely he is to Dorothea, and later, via Mr Brooke, asks if he may approach Dorothea with a view to marriage. He writes her a letter of proposal, and she replies accepting him. Her sister Celia is disgusted, as is Sir James Chettam, who had hoped to marry her himself. He learns of the forth-coming marriage from the sharp-tongued Mrs Cadwallader, wife of a neigh-bouring Rector, while Dorothea continues with her thoughts of how best she can become a practical and supportive helpmeet to her erudite hus-band. Sir James begins to pay 'small attentions' to Celia. Soon Dorothea visits Lowick, Casaubon's home, and there meets the latter's cousin, Will Ladislaw.

Mr Brooke, as a prospective Parliamentary candidate for Middlemarch, gives a dinner party where the gathering includes Mr Bulstrode the banker, Lady Chettam, Mrs Cadwallader and the new young doctor, Lydgate. Some retrospect on the latter reveals his interest in Rosamond Vincy, daughter of the coming Mayor of Middlemarch, and brings into the narra-tive her brother Fred, whose uncle, the dying Peter Featherstone, of Stone Court, may leave him some money. Fred and Rosamond visit Stone Court, where Mary Garth (with whom Fred is in love) is in attendance on the old man. Peter Featherstone interrogates Fred about his having borrowed money on the strength of his expectations, Bulstrode being the source of his information. Lydgate calls to see his patient, and Rosamond feels that she has fallen in love with the doctor.

Commentary

Chapter 1
The bald summary above covers the first 12 chapters of the novel. At once we are made aware of the contrast between the two sisters, with Dorothea, not yet twenty, the idealist, and Celia the practically-minded down-to-earth character whose 'pretty carnally-minded prose' is capable of bringing Dorothea down-to-earth too. The author's irony is tolerant but revealing. Thus we are told that Dorothea loved riding 'in a pagan, sensuous way, and always looked forward to renouncing it'.

Particularly revealing is the two sisters' discussion of their mother's jewels. Celia is fascinated by them and longs to wear them for display. The contrast is enhanced by the clear insight we are given into Dorothea's motives and her attendant lack of self-knowledge. The irony plays over the dialogue, which is convincing, natural and unforced, but authorial com-mentary on the characters sustains the division between illusion and reality which is central to Dorothea's character. She does not know that Sir James is in love with her; she thinks in terms of cottages for sick labourers rather than of men appreciating her as a woman. Significantly, the motto to the first chapter is from Beaumont and Fletcher's *The Maid's Tragedy*, the title of that Jacobean play forecasting Dorothea's future lot. This is the depth at which George Eliot works; her feeling for total relevance makes the mottoes to her chapters an extension of the text. But George Eliot is careful too to give an exact historical placement, since *Middlemarch* is set in real, significant time, and she mentions 'Mr Peel's late conduct on the Catholic question', a reference to the Bill for Catholic Emancipation which was passed in 1829.

Chapter 2

The dinner-party in chapter 2 is rich in humour, the comedy of interaction, the insight into what is superficial running with the unvoiced thoughts which go deep. Mr Brooke's bumbling conversation, his name-dropping capacity, his inability to carry an argument through to its conclusion, all these are given a considered stress, not without its irony since this is our first introduction to a prospective Parliamentary candidate. He is also mean, and we notice that it is Dorothea who has the reforming zeal. Casaubon's first utterance reveals the man: it is sententious and pathetic, showing his deprivation, its 'sing-song neatness' impressing Dorothea, who feels that she would like to be a 'lamp-holder' to this 'ghost of an ancient' as he tries to reconstruct the world of the past. It is the first of the light images in the novel, these ranging from the taper supposedly carried by Casaubon as he follows out his 'mouldy futilities' to the sun which irradiates Ladislaw's voice and laugh.

Dorothea's illusions are conveyed through her exaggerated attentions to Casaubon and her impatience with Sir James as well as her defence of her self-mortification over giving up riding. Mr Brooke's superficiality is indicated when we are told that 'the remark lay in his mind as lightly as the broken wing of an insect'. By a subtle irony Mr Brooke's references – to Sir Humphry Davy and 'the poet Wordsworth, you know' – are complemented by Dorothea's serious analogy of Casaubon resembling the philosopher John Locke. Again the division between illusion and reality is being stressed, as Sir James pays attention to Dorothea and thinks that he knows her. And here the author's irony embraces the so-called superiority of the male who 'has always the advantage of being masculine -. . and even his ignorance is of a sounder quality'. The tone embraces Casaubon's speech – 'We must keep the germinating grain away from the light' – and Dorothea's illusion in 'Has any one ever pinched into its pilulous smallness the cobweb of pre-matrimonial acquaintanceship?'

Chapter 3

The ironic contemplation of the developing relationship between Casaubon and Dorothea is continued. The motto is from Milton's *Paradise Lost*, the Eve of the poem reflecting the essential gullibility of Dorothea and the Raphael the 'archangelic manner' of Casaubon. The imagery is ironic too, for reasons had 'budded and bloomed' and Casaubon will gather 'this great harvest of truth'. Dorothea 'had looked deep into the ungauged reservoir of Mr Casaubon's mind' and he feels his work 'luminous with the reflected light of correspondences'. The key word, however, is 'labyrinthine', with its implications of a maze from which one cannot escape, whether it be the work or, subtly hinted here, the responsibilities of marriage. The skipping superficiality of Mr Brooke's acquaintance with Greece offsets the intimate knowledge of the pagan world held by his 'somewhat sad audience', Casaubon. The latter's face 'was often lit up by a smile like pale wintry sunshine', but the author parodies Casaubon's own methods of annotation and conversation in appropriate prose inlaid with appropriate quotations.

When Casaubon leaves, the full-bloodedness (though she herself is unaware of it) of Dorothea is stressed, but at the same time the deprived nature of her narrow existence is indicated – and subtly – by the unifying imagery we noticed earlier in the chapter, for she faces 'a labyrinth of petty courses, a walled-in maze of small paths that led no whither'. This shows George Eliot's awareness of structure, her tight control over her material, for this image sets up a resonance in the reader's mind. It is, too, prophetically appropriate to the nature of Casaubon's work. In the course of this chapter Casaubon is compared to Bossuet, Augustine and then Pascal, all great men (which he is not), but all underlining that quality of Dorothea's blindness to reality; books and theories are no substitute for life experience. Her reverie interrupted by the innocent Sir James, Dorothea reveals herself as not so saintly as to be able to overcome impulse. George Eliot is also drawing an obvious contrast between the young and healthy Sir James and the prematurely old and arid Casaubon. While Sir James enjoys his illusions that he is making progress with Dorothea, Dorothea confirms her own impressions after more conversations with Casaubon. The deadness of the latter is silently emphasised by the imagery; what he says seems 'like a specimen from a mine, or the inscription on the door of a museum'. His way of life is the aridly verbal rather than the vibrant – 'He assented to her expressions of devout feeling, and usually with an appropriate quotation', but their future incompatibility is foreshadowed in his indifference to the plans for labourers' cottages.

Chapter 4

Dorothea, who is to have many encounters with truth, has her first taste of it when Celia points out that it is she (Dorothea) with whom Sir James is in love. Dorothea is so impressionable (and perhaps a little guilty) that she is moved to tears of revulsion. Celia tells her sister, 'You always see what nobody else sees; it is impossible to satisfy you; yet you never see what is quite plain.' Celia *does* see what is quite plain, and perhaps there is a degree of malice in her choosing to call her sister 'Dodo'. Mr Brooke's bringing pamphlets about the early Church produces an image of the 'electric stream' and, heavily ironic, 'the scent of a fresh bouquet' to explain Dorothea's complete change of mood at the prospect of reading Casaubon's marginalia. Already she has moved away from life again, for she is almost indifferent to the fact that a sheep-stealer is to be hanged. In typical 'labyrinthine' Brooke style her uncle gradually gets round to the fact that Casaubon has told him he wishes to marry Dorothea, and his meanness and practicality are shown by his still pressing the claims of Chettam – after all, 'our land lies together'. With a lack of feeling (though he is concerned for Dorothea's happiness) he uses the 'noose' image to describe marriage, thus unconsciously evoking the sheep-stealer who is to lose his life. Dorothea's life – and Casaubon's at this stage – are illusions. Mr Brooke's own inadequacies and failure to cope with life are finely expressed at the end of this chapter. Yet, as always, he has an eye to the main chance, considering that Casaubon may become a bishop.

Chapter 5
Casaubon's letter is self-conscious, pedantic, sententious, totally lacking in passion. Even his chosen images – 'sequel' 'no backward pages whereon' – are a consonant with his concern for words rather than life. Dorothea's reaction – she sobs – shows the depth of passionate feeling within her which she does not understand. The author's imagery – 'she was a neophyte about to enter on a higher grade of initiation' – shows how blind (and ignorant) Dorothea is of the flesh as compared with the spirit. Dorothea's own letter provides the contrast to Casaubon's with its naïve, simple, direct expression of devotion – the word that she would undoubtedly have chosen as a synonym for love. Narrative dramatic irony is used when the sisters are together on the evening of the proposal, with Celia in ignorance of it. Particularly effective is the contrast, with Dorothea reacting affectionately, 'gravely' and 'fervently'. While Dorothea is moving towards her confession to her sister, she contemplates 'the great cedar silvered with the damp', a fine symbolic anticipation of Dorothea's blighted life to come. Celia provokes the confession by her own description of Mr Casaubon in the cold light of day (as distinct from the warm glow of illusion). George Eliot notes her reaction to it by a telling focus on her practical nature – 'The paper man she was making would have had his leg injured, but for her habitual care of whatever she held in her hands.' Dorothea, however, becomes aware that her forthcoming marriage may attract adverse comment; her immediate compensation comes with Casaubon's visit that same evening, his rather hackneyed,'I have been little disposed to gather flowers . . . I shall pluck them with eagerness, to place them in your bosom' being defined by the author as 'frigid rhetoric' and 'the cawing of an amorous rook'. Further authorial irony categorises Casaubon as a 'Protestant Pope'.

Chapter 6
Mrs Cadwallader has a choric function when she appears in *Middlemarch*, and the motto to the chapter – written by George Eliot herself – underlines this. Her first exchange, with Mrs Fitchett, displays her sharp bargaining capacity; skinflint she has to be, but she carries it through with a generosity of spirit absent in Mr Brooke. She adopts a vividly satirical tone towards Mr Brooke, anticipating him being 'burnt in effigy this 5th of November coming'. By a sublime stroke of irony later George Eliot has an effigy of him produced during his first speech for nomination which effectively destroys his candidature. Mr Brooke cannot stand private or public ridicule. Mrs Cadwallader's 'Nice cutting' actually contains a prophetic sketch of Mr Brooke as a failed politician. Her sharpness soon uncovers the news about Dorothea, but the comedy of Mr Brooke's retreat is covered by the arrival of Celia, who tells the truth.

Mrs Cadwallader's verbal wit is employed to good account, as she considers that Casaubon's 'family quarterings are three cuttle-fish sable, and a commentator rampant'. She proceeds straight to give Sir James the news, prefacing it with a little blackmail over Mr Brooke standing as a Liberal for

Middlemarch. To Mrs Cadwallader, Casaubon's soul is 'A great bladder for dried peas to rattle in', while to Sir James he is a 'mummy'. Mrs Cadwallader immediately adapts her matchmaking motives by suggesting that Sir James is well rid of Dorothea and should turn his attentions to Celia. The author's voice is well in evidence in extenuation of Mrs Cadwallader, and we notice her own scientific bent in the analogies with the microscope and the lens as well as the broader aerial sweep of the telescope. Important is the social placing of Mrs Cadwallader, with her 'excellent pickle of epigrams' and her hatred of the 'vulgar rich'. It is a superb piece of individual characterisation. The effect of her words about Celia to Sir James causes him to be thankful that he has not actually proposed to Dorothea, and the authorial voice rounds off his reaction neatly by observing that 'We mortals, men and women, devour many a disappointment between breakfast and dinner-time.'

Chapter 7
Water imagery is used to indicate the moderate abandonment of Casaubon to the experience of love – 'the stream of feeling' is only a 'shallow rill', and he cannot undertake a 'plunge'. These images obviously carry sexual overtones and indicate that Casaubon is perhaps impotent. Dorothea, offering to read 'Latin and Greek aloud to you, as Milton's daughters did to their father', is unconsciously making her first inroads into Casaubon's life which are to prove so mutually embarrassing to them both later. Mr Brooke reveals his own views on what the limits of a woman's education should be, views which today would be called chauvinistic. Dorothea shows her emotional impressionability once more by admitting that the great organ at Freiberg made her sob, and the author enjoys a further ironic look at Mr Brooke, saying 'it is a very narrow mind which cannot look at a subject from various points of view'.

Chapter 8
The chapter motto underlines Sir James's intention of saving Dorothea from Casaubon, though his reaction that he has not been eclipsed by a brilliant rival is tinctured with a determination to try to prevent the match. His turning to Cadwallader is natural enough, but Cadwallader is a man of strong good sense, even welcoming Mr Brooke's candidature as a Whig since it could only strengthen Conservatism. He also redresses the balance somewhat on Casaubon's side, pointing out the good things he has done, like educating Will Ladislaw, for example. With the entrance of Mrs Cadwallader the 'cutting edge' is resumed, for she describes Casaubon's blood as 'all semicolons and parentheses'. There is a very interesting moral corollary running throughout this chapter, with Sir James and Mrs Cadwallader insisting that Dorothea will be unhappy, and Cadwallader equally strongly urging her freedom to choose. The Rector has the kind of wit which shows how well-matched he is with his wife, and we are told that 'He always saw the joke of any satire against himself'. The essential goodness of Sir James is shown by the way he continues to devote himself to Dorothea's plans for the cottages and, humanly, his gradual movement

towards the less complicated Celia.

Chapter 9

Dorothea's first visit to Lowick is made on 'a grey but dry November morning'. The description of the house foreshadows the future, with words like 'melancholy', 'confined' and 'sombre' hinting at the emotional and mental prison awaiting Dorothea. A telling emphasis suggests that the house should have children, and again we think of Dorothea and her 'maternal' hands. George Eliot's reticence, her use of analogy of this kind to suggest deprivation, shows us how carefully she is preparing for the marriage of Dorothea and Casaubon. Celia, by contrast, indulges a little fantasy about Sir James 'like a prince issuing from his enchantment in a rose-bush' at Freshitt Hall. Dorothea reacts, as one would expect, to the 'autumnal decline' of the house by liking everything that she sees, typically considering that it is all 'hallowed'. The irony is that she fills all the 'blanks' with 'happy assurance'. The provision of a separate 'boudoir' for Dorothea, together with the description of 'A piece of tapestry over a door also showed a blue-green world with a pale stag in it', hint at her unsexual existence to come.

Mr Casaubon's revelation that his aunt had made a bad marriage prepares us for his treatment of Will – duty obliges him to help but not to show warmth – so that an important plot segment is fitted in here. Will, grandson of the aunt mentioned by Casaubon, is fully described, but his 'pouting air of discontent' and his 'colouring, perhaps with temper rather than modesty' do not ring true. Mr Brooke's inconsequential chatter involves an invitation to Ladislaw to visit him – this too is to carry its positive ramifications in the plot – and the entry into Ladislaw's consciousness shows him romantically smitten with Dorothea almost before he has had time to think. Again his registering of her effect on him smacks of hyperbole, for Dorothea has 'the voice of a soul that had once lived in an Aeolian harp'. Afterwards his face is 'lit up' as he laughs at himself, partly because of Mr Brooke but also at the prospect of Casaubon marrying Dorothea. Casaubon's severity is shown in his account of Will's career and failure to stick to a profession, and prepares us for his jealous severity later. The plot link also prepares us for Will's reappearance in Rome, for we learn that Casaubon is to allow him sufficient means to go to Italy.

Chapter 10

Will must have his freedom, but it is given in authorial account rather than convincingly from Will's own consciousness. The imagery does not help, the world having 'handsome dubious eggs called possibilities' while Will ponders on 'long incubation producing no chick'. A long, omniscient pronouncement warns the reader against accepting opinions about Mr Casaubon – presumably this is going some way to redress our sympathy for him – and takes on perspective by observing that 'Milton, looking for his portrait in a spoon, must submit to have the facial angle of a bumpkin.' This is the prelude to a sympathetic identification with Casaubon; imagery of flowers is used to convey what his marriage should be like, though he prefers 'the accustomed vaults where he walked taper in hand'. This muted light imagery is reinforced by the distance of financial imagery. Casaubon believes that his bachelorhood 'had stored up for him a compound interest of enjoyment'. The fact is that Casaubon is lonely, insecure, frustrated in his work, while Dorothea believes that *he* will bring her life into contact with the past and give it meaning

A reference to St Theresa underlines Dorothea's ardour, and the lamp imagery is used once more as pathetic emphasis of Dorothea's illusion. The incompatibility is shown in Casaubon's wishing to take Celia with them on their honeymoon, for Casaubon does not realise that he has hurt Dorothea. The latter recovers in the certain knowledge that her husband is so far above her 'that he needs me less than I need him'. The second part of this chapter is important in the structure of the novel. The dinner-party is held at the Grange, but it marks a move into Middlemarch society, prefigures Mr Brooke's candidature, and thus is a considered expansion into a wider area, with characters who will play significant roles in the action of *Middlemarch* appearing for the first time.

It moves, if you like, from the small world of individual consciousnesses into the larger world in which public experience – which conditions private lives – has its being. The presentation is ironic, occasionally satirical, as with the lawyer Mr Standish, who 'had become landed himself'. Mr Bulstrode is obviously narrow, and the mention of Rosamond Vincy, not at the party, indicates the fine gradations of class which exist in pre-Reform Middlemarch. The women talk about their health and doctors – fine witty observation this on the part of the author – as prelude to the introduction of Lydgate, but Mrs Cadwallader manages to be acidic on the subject of Casaubon ('he looks like a death's head skinned over for the occasion') and prophetic ('in a year from this time that girl will hate him'). Lydgate has the advantage of breeding, refinement, 'of looking perfectly grave', a kind of superior social manner, saying ' "I think so" with an air of so much deference accompanying the insight of agreement'. Important to the plot is Bulstrode's determination to give Lydgate management of the new hospital, the resistance already apparent to Bulstrode, and Lydgate's own judgement of Dorothea as 'a little too earnest'.

Chapter 11

There is retrospect on Lydgate, revealing his susceptibility to the 'true melodic charm' of Rosamond Vincy. He intends to remain a bachelor, is 'young, poor, ambitious', and in contrasting him with Casaubon, George Eliot stresses 'the stealthy convergence of human lots' and thus indicates her own narrative technique of interaction. As she puts it, 'Destiny stands by sarcastic with our dramatis personae folded in her hand.' A brilliant sense of perspective establishes the mores of 'Old provincial society', with its slight shiftings and 'threads of connection', with 'settlers' like Lydgate arriving and contributing their own small share of change. The irony finally settles on Rosamond, with a delicious sense of superficiality; she was 'the flower of Mrs Lemon's school', noted for the propriety of her speech and her superior musical accomplishments.

Rosamond's finicky nature is reflected in the matter of the herrings and in her ·pulling up her mother for saying 'the pick of them'. Fred enters late but effectively with the assertion that 'correct English is the slang of prigs who write history and essays' and he is also satirical about Rosamond's evident snobbery, defining it as 'certain finicking notions which are the classics of Mrs Lemon's school'. Fred also retails news of Lydgate, Rosamond reveals a capacity to hurt Fred by referring to Mary Garth and, ever aware of the need to push her children forward for money, Mrs Vincy urges Rosamond to visit her sick uncle, Peter Featherstone. Rosamond, by indulging Fred, shows her cunning; she wants to go to Stone Court with him the next day, not so much to see her uncle, but in the hope of seeing Lydgate. George Eliot is superb at family interiors, and here we have the naturalness of family interaction – pride, humour, jealousy, love and pettiness. Rosamond is emerging as a cunning egoist.

Chapter 12
The ride to Stone Court is traced with a loving emphasis on 'roots', each field having 'a particular physiognomy'. Mrs Waule, mindful of a possible legacy, is busy stirring things up against Fred with Peter Featherstone. The latter is sharp and mindful too of motives – a freshly minted character – and George Eliot captures superbly a contrasting family interaction, with a moral emphasis on greed and gossip. Peter Featherstone can be blunt – he dismisses Mrs Waule, whose 'muffled monotone' is pathetic and comic – and direct, as he is with Fred. The latter is made to feel guilty – a measure of his conscience, to be abundantly demonstrated later – and old Featherstone enjoys his exertion of power by demanding that Bulstrode provide a written denial. He also has an unconscious prophetic streak, saying of Bulstrode that 'He may come down any day, when the devil leaves off backing him.' He also asserts the power of property as against that of speculation. Fred, growing more human if weak and fallible every minute, feels pity for the old man, who is in fact tyrannical to Mary Garth, forbidding her books since they may take her attention away from him. Yet such is George Eliot's power of characterisation that we too feel pity for this old man who only has companionship near his death because he has money.

While Featherstone is with Fred, George Eliot draws a fine contrast between the sexually attractive 'angel' Rosamond and the 'ordinary sinner' Mary Garth, whose life is given to service and duty. Yet she has a streak of 'satiric bitterness' which balances her honesty and her capacity to laugh at herself. Rosamond deftly turns the conversation to Lydgate, but Mary sees through the manœuvre, 'not choosing to indulge Rosamond's indirectness'. She also sees through Lydgate, who hasn't deigned to notice her, and engages in a moral debate with Rosamond about Fred's unfitness to enter the church. Mary's skill in argument, the honesty referred to above, and a quality of integrity – unlike Rosamond, she is herself and not an actress – and her knowledge that the Vincys would *not* like her to marry Fred, all these make her intensely and interestingly human.

Lydgate's arrival gives Featherstone a chance to show Rosamond off and Rosamond a chance to move Lydgate by the quality of her (simulated) kindness to Mary. Romance has come for Rosamond, and the imagery ('her flower-like head on its white stem') is thus at one remove from reality. She is equal to the situation which she has foreseen will develop ('she even acted her own character, and so well, that she did not know it to be precisely her own'). A fine symbolic moment has Lydgate picking up the whip for Rosamond, and their eyes meeting; ironically, Lydgate himself is to be scourged by their marriage. Rosamond has contrived this, but finds that 'reality proved much more moving than anticipation'. There is a fine contrast in the final section of the chapter, with Rosamond's fantasies busy with an elevated future, and Fred's absorbed by the embarrassing present of how to get the denial from Bulstrode.

BOOK II   OLD AND YOUNG

Summary

Bulstrode and Lydgate discuss the possibility of hospital improvement before Mr Vincy tries to get the important denial out of Bulstrode. They argue, but Bulstrode (married to Mr Vincy's sister) agrees to consider giving Vincy the letter which will clear Fred of borrowing money. He does, sends the letter, and Fred takes it to Peter Featherstone, who gives him money, though not as much as he had hoped for. After seeing Mary, Fred asks his mother to take care of £80 for him. The focus switches to Lydgate, his knowledge, his ideals, his weaknesses, the state of medicine and his past infatuation for an actress, Laure. The chaplaincy of the hospital is shortly to be voted on, with Bulstrode backing the candidature of Mr Tyke and some of the others backing the pleasantly acceptable but not so devout Mr Farebrother. Lydgate and Rosamond meet, but each is unaware of what the other is thinking.

Mr Farebrother is introduced, Lydgate visits him, and they discuss Bulstrode and various Middlemarchers. Shortly after this comes the vote on the chaplaincy question, Lydgate's vote for Tyke in support of Bulstrode ensuring that Tyke and not Farebrother is appointed. The narrative moves to Rome, with Ladislaw and his artist friend Naumann. The latter is intent on painting Dorothea, who is in Rome on her honeymoon. We soon learn that Dorothea is very unhappy, anxious to help her husband, but that Casaubon jealously guards his work from her. When Ladislaw visits her he tells her that her husband's researches are limited. Casaubon himself is uneasy and weary, and the strains of marriage are revealing themselves. Meanwhile Will contrives a meeting between Naumann and Dorothea, and the artist flatters Casaubon by telling him that he wishes to paint him as St Thomas Aquinas. Will and Dorothea have a debate about art, poetry and life, but afterwards Casaubon says that he does not wish to discuss Will.

Commentary

Chapter 13

Bulstrode is described, his sickliness and bearing making his listeners feel that a 'moral lantern' is being turned on them. Note too the deliberate air of mystery surrounding him – another stranger, like Lydgate – who had come to Middlemarch some years ago. It is an important hint of the plot revelations to come; this early Bulstrode and Lydgate are identified with each other over the affair of Tyke, whereas in the final stages of the novel they are to be seen – by Middlemarchers – as being in criminal conspiracy. Here we can compare the two men, with Bulstrode conscious of patronage and Lydgate intent on practical application of his ideals.

Bulstrode is equally intent on stressing the spiritual health of the sick, and proceeds to indoctrinate Lydgate against Farebrother – 'a man deeply painful to contemplate'. Lydgate in response is 'bent on being circumspect', but Bulstrode reveals the strength of his feelings and a deep-rooted insecurity, even something of a persecution complex. Fate intervenes in the person of the florid Mr Vincy, whose openness contrasts with the rigid moral and spiritual stance taken by Bulstrode. Again we note the naturalness of the dialogue, with Vincy driven by Bulstrode's self-righteousness to condemn the latter's 'tyrannical spirit'. Vincy's simple morality and bluntness allow him more than a passing snipe at Bulstrode – 'you must be first chop in heaven, else you won't like it much' – but his creed is that families should stick together. The light/mirror imagery is used to reveal to Bulstrode his own lack of generosity, for he sees 'a very unsatisfactory reflection of himself in the coarse unflattering mirror which that manufacturer's [Vincy's] mind presented to the subtler lights and shadows of his fellow-men'.

Chapter 14

The motto is centrally focused on Bulstrode and hints at the revelations of the past to come. The letter is finely satirised by Peter Featherstone for its aridly inflated language; his own language to Mary Garth is selfish and blunt, and we are made aware of the extent of her daily suffering. Old Featherstone is adept at playing off his relations against each other, and enjoys keeping Fred in suspense over the amount of money he is going to give him; his actions here anticipate his various changes of mind and the successive wills later, a mark of consistency in his presentation. He enjoys power.

Fred, despite his disappointment over the amount of money he gets, has conscience enough to be 'a little ashamed before his inner self', again a mark of his moral reclamation to come. Mary soon recovers from passing self-pity, and reveals a delightful sense of humour. She baits Fred somewhat on not having chosen a positive course of action (note the structural parallel with Ladislaw), but draws humorous parallels to their situation from literature. Her eyes are compared to 'clear windows', an image which is equated with looking outward – giving to others – by contrast with the mirror images which abound in *Middlemarch*, and which reflect egoism.

The exchange between them is poignant with Fred's suffering and Mary's morally responsible stance. The chapter ends on a note of dramatic tension with the revelation that Fred owes Mr Garth money.

Chapter 15

This opens with an important omniscient comment as the author cautions herself against a too long interruption of the narrative, taking the example of Henry Fielding, the eighteenth-century novelist. The imagery stresses the social and moral interaction of her characters – 'seeing how they were woven and interwoven' – the image of 'this particular web' being central to her own conception (note the distinction between the web and maze/labyrinthine images, for the web is carefully constructed, like the novel, and is complete in itself). Lydgate is referred to as a 'settler', an image which is to be invoked later, and the object of the retrospect on him is to integrate him, psychologically and professionally, in his time. His discovery of anatomy determines his future bent, but there is some fine irony on the nature of a 'liberal education' and a strong focus on his acquiring an 'intellectual passion'.

A disquisition (unconsciously ironic in view of the opening of the chapter) on failed idealists (a structural link with Dorothea) is prelude to deeper investigation of Lydgate, whose coming susceptibility is fore-shadowed in 'He cared not only for "cases", but for John and Elizabeth, especially Elizabeth.' The structural balance of the novel is further shown here by the documentation of the need for medical reform which parallels the political reform which is a running theme in *Middlemarch*. Lydgate's dedication and ambitions are clearly indicated in this 'dark period' of medical history, for he means to make 'a link in the chain of discovery'. Lydgate is also intent on being practically independent, for he would 'simply prescribe, without dispensing drugs or taking percentage from druggists'.

His vision is abundantly indicated by the imagery – 'discoverer', 'about 1829 the dark territories of Pathology were a fine America for a spirited young adventurer' – and also by George Eliot's sure scientific grasp. Lydgate's own ambitions are summed up in the phrase that he wished 'to do good small work for Middlemarch and great work for the world'. But he is fallible, 'a little spotted with commonness', has an arrogant conceit, and is 'benevolently contemptuous'. He – like Dorothea – is blind to certain effects and issues, and the account of his infatuation with the actress Laure is meant to illustrate his emotional frailty. It does, but lacks the realism and immediacy which are the main features of the narrative. It underlines his susceptibility, and prepares us for his sudden succumbing to Rosamond.

Chapter 16

The question of the chaplaincy again underlines the structural links being established between the small world and the great, this political decision mirroring the wider political decisions being taken at the time. There is reference to Bulstrode being a 'ruler' though faced with 'an opposition party', imagery which is tellingly extended in Chapter 18. The switch to the dinner-party at Vincy's (a subtle duplication of the dinner-party in Book I) enables us to see Lydgate in interaction with his fellows, one of whom, the coroner, he manages to offend by his uncompromising (and insensitive) views. We also see him in interaction with Rosamond, the imagery used of the latter being appropriately, if ironically, romantic, 'as if the petals of some gigantic flower had just opened and disclosed her'. Her kittenish qualities fascinate Lydgate, though the authorial irony observes that 'she was a sylph caught young and educated at Mrs Lemon's'. She further fascinates Lydgate by her piano playing, but he is (as he thinks) equally interested in Mr Farebrother, who 'came like a pleasant change in the light'.

Lydgate's lack of awareness about himself – his complete ignorance of what Rosamond is thinking about and her motivations – gives way to 'a triumphant delight in his studies'. Rosamond, of course, has 'registered every look and word' of Lydgate's, and the structural parallels with the Casaubon/Dorothea ignorance of each other are being delved here. Rosamond has the ability 'to discern very subtly the faintest aroma of rank'. But the emphasis is on the dissonance of appearance and reality, Rosamond always having 'an audience in her own consciousness'. The subtle investigation of this chapter is of consciousness in depth; there is a remarkable individualising, the reader seeing what the characters cannot see and which will only be revealed to them by that most exacting of all experiences, marriage.

Chapter 17

This opens with a fine interior of Mr Farebrother's house and a succinctly observed description of his family. These are character etchings, but not caricatures, each one having a distinct individuality and, in the case of Henrietta Noble, eccentricity. We note the moral index; Miss Noble gives to the poor. Mrs Farebrother, the mother, has proverbialisms at will, observing 'When you get me a good man made out of arguments, I will get you a good dinner with reading you the cookery-book.' She is aggressive on her son's account and dismissive of Tyke. Farebrother reveals his own casual expertise in entomology, while Lydgate uses an image of himself and his studies in structure which is associated with the 'explorer' conception, namely 'I have the sea to swim in there.'

In a brilliantly witty passage Farebrother reveals that he has probably missed his vocation, yet ironically what he says, for example about 'a learned treatise on the entomology of the Pentateuch', and much like this, is almost an unconscious parody of Casaubon's researches – and thus another structural parallel. Farebrother talks good sense, and reveals his own interest in Mary Garth (who, we remember, was scarcely noticed by Lydgate). He also says, and in view of what is to come we note the irony – 'a good unworldly woman – may really help a man'. He has himself in mind, but the words assuredly apply to Lydgate. Farebrother defines Bulstrode's limitations and his 'worldly-spiritual cliqueism', but it is done without malice. He also reveals a generosity of spirit, for even if Lydgate does not vote for him he wants to keep him as a friend.

Chapter 18

The blank verse motto to the chapter reflects Lydgate as explorer with spots of commonness, the disease imagery indicative of the latter. Lydgate has a profoundly sympathetic view of Farebrother, whom he finds 'sweet-tempered, ready-witted, frank', but decision is upon him. Lydgate thinks in the political imagery we have noted earlier – 'He could not help hearing within him the distinct declaration that Bulstrode was prime minister, and that the Tyke affair was a question of office or no office', the 'petty politics' mirroring the wider politics of reform (and note that the hospital itself is a measure of reform). Farebrother's gambling is one of his spots of commonness, and Lydgate convinces himself of the importance of this; he winces, thinks that he could act independently of Bulstrode, but does not do so.

Lydgate's weakness, his susceptibility to the moment and the convenient choice, is consistently presented. He feels 'the hampering threadlike pressure of small social conditions' (an image obviously derived from the web). The narrative moves to a contemplation of the others involved in the decision; again we are aware of the continuing political analogy (Dr Sprague is compared to the Lord Chancellor). The temperature and the temper of the discussion are graphically recorded, the delay in the entrance of Lydgate a fine dramatic stroke which maintains the tension. Mr Brooke is his typical vacillating self, but with the votes evenly split there is conclusive drama as Lydgate votes. The irony over his decision to vote for Tyke is that he will now be identified with Bulstrode in the much greater crisis to come. More irony at the end of the chapter carries another implication: 'Lydgate thought that there was a pitiable infirmity of will in Mr Farebrother', but the phrase appropriately defines his own weakness.

Chapter 19

The superb opening sentence conveys a sense of historical and personal perspective, that linking of the public life with the private life which is at the heart of George Eliot's fiction. Dorothea is seen against the great examples of pagan sensuous art, her 'Quakerish grey drapery' contrasting with the 'marble voluptuousness' of the Ariadne. Her eyes are 'fixed dreamily on a streak of sunlight which fell across the floor'. This is brilliantly compressed writing conveying, as it does, the unawakened Dorothea, what the artist Naumann here calls 'sensuous force controlled by spiritual passion'. Will is irritated, but breaks into 'sunshiny laughter' – a reflection of the 'streak of sunlight' – representing warmth and the life-giving force so absent in Casaubon. Will considers language superior to art, but Naumann is acute enough to penetrate Will's emergent possessiveness over Dorothea.

Chapter 20
This chapter is a moving description of the beginning of positive incompatibility between Dorothea and Casaubon. The motto aptly defines Dorothea – a child who needs love, and prepares us for the crisis which finds her weeping. In a word, Dorothea is desolate, bewildered by the fragmentary nature of her experiences in Rome and the 'dream-like strangeness of her bridal life'. It is a fine phrase to define her deprivation, emotional and sexual, for characteristically she likes to 'feel alone with the earth and sky'. A superb description of the effect of Rome on her, the collossal impact of art and religion, the degraded past and the 'sordid present', is reinforced by an omniscient comment on human vulnerability:

> If we had a keen vision and feeling of all ordinary human life, it would be like hearing the grass grow and the squirrel's heart beat, and we should die of that roar which lies on the other side of silence.

Again the image of water is used to describe the critical early period in a marriage, 'whether that of a shrimp-pool or of deeper waters' as well as the light, which now has 'changed, and you cannot find the pearly dawn at noonday'. For Dorothea the 'wide fresh air' has been replaced by 'anterooms and winding passages which seemed to lead nowhither'. Note that this is the image of the maze or labyrinth again, and that it is definitive of Casaubon's work and, poignantly now, of Dorothea's life. The constrictions are further emphasised by the reference to the 'marital voyage . . . the sea is not within sight . . . you are exploring an enclosed basin'. Dorothea is irritated by her husband's comments on the rich experiences of Rome (bewildering to her), feeling a 'mental shiver' at his lack of involved response, at his 'lifeless embalmment of knowledge'. One fine sentence links Casaubon comprehensively with the main imagery sequences of the novel:

> With his taper stuck before him he forgot the absence of windows, and in bitter manuscript remarks on other men's notions about the solar deities, he had become indifferent to the sunlight.

Dorothea longs for expressed affection which it is beyond Casaubon to give. Her 'ideas and resolves seemed like melting ice floating and lost in the warm flood of which they had been but another form'. Casaubon's blindness to her needs is shown in his pedantically epigrammatic, 'See Rome as a bride, and live henceforth as a happy wife.' The wife is unhappy, mindful of the evenings when Casaubon has been unable to 'surface' (George Eliot's word) into life. Dorothea, however, probes Casaubon about the completion of his work, and here we see her blindness to his 'inward troubles'. For just as Casaubon is an arid man, so his work is arid too, and he is sensitive about its non-completion, jealously guarding his secret and now, incomprehensibly, finding his partner the chief spy. His rejection of Dorothea's closeness on this issue, a reply informed with scholarly passion, leads to anger, and 'Both were shocked at their mutual situation.' None the less the authorial comment at the end of the chapter indicates Dorothea's fullness of nature, the 'reaching forward of the whole consciousness towards the fullest truth, the least partial good'.

Chapter 21

Dorothea's frankness, openness and resilience are shown in her greeting of Will. The latter, to his own surprise, is impressionable enough to be initially shy. Although she shows 'the quietude of a benignant matron' there are also 'signs of girlish sorrow', but we note Dorothea's strength of character in immediately responding to Will's needs and putting aside her own. Will's impetuous and volatile nature is shown in the reaction – which he controls into a smile – to Casaubon groping after his 'mouldy futilities' and leaving Dorothea alone. Dorothea is delightfully (endearingly to Will) modest about her own lack of art appreciation, and Will responds with a like frankness about his own inability to settle to anything. Their exchange is punctuated by Will's dislike of Casaubon and Dorothea's defensive attitude about her husband. Will does not spare Casaubon's lack of knowledge of German criticism, saying by innuendo that he is 'groping about in woods with a pocket-compass while they have made good roads'.

There is a sharp transition from Will's imagination to Casaubon's entrance, and the now familiar imagery of 'sunny brightness' for Will is balanced by the statement that Casaubon 'stood rayless'. When Will leaves, Dorothea asks for her husband's forgiveness; he gives it, but it is lacking in warmth of feeling, the kind of forgiveness that only adds to the distance. We note, however, that although his jealousy is a 'blight bred in the cloudy, damp despondency of uneasy egoism' he has the sensitivity to refrain from telling Dorothea that she shouldn't have received Will in his absence. Dorothea is growing in insight, painful though it is, recognising that her husband 'had an equivalent centre of self'.

Chapter 22

Will puts himself out to please Casaubon, but, we suspect, to please Dorothea more, and cunningly injects into the conversation the idea that they should visit a studio. He guides them to Naumann's, the jokes being rather too much for Casaubon, who is sensitive enough to feel that he is being laughed at. The deception is continued by Naumann, who, wishing to paint Dorothea, first suggests that Casaubon would make a good St Thomas Aquinas (Casaubon's looks 'improved with a glow of delight'). Will's impetuosity is scarcely under control when Naumann asks Dorothea to be a model as Santa Clara and has the impudence (Will's word) to adjust her arm. We notice the increased rate of Will's ardour towards Dorothea, the irony being that in her innocence she has no awareness of it. Casaubon, with understandable vanity, arranges to buy the picture of himself; later Will and Naumann discuss Casaubon, Will observing with some temper and not a little jealousy that 'He's a cursed white-blooded pedantic coxcomb.' Although this is characteristic hyperbole, we recognise that George Eliot has further humanised Will by making him something of a hypocrite in propitiating Casaubon so that Dorothea could be painted by his friend. His anxiety to have Dorothea remember him as someone special is also human; he contrives to visit her alone, and Dorothea's simplicity, modesty, freedom from artifice come across when they discuss art. She observes that 'all this expense of art, that seems somehow to lie outside life and make it no better for the world, pains one'. This naïvety underlines the consistency in the presentation of Dorothea.

Will, with passion and prophecy, thinks of Dorothea as 'shut up in that stone prison at Lowick'. Dorothea is unaware of his passion, intent still on finding out what her husband needs to do in order to bring about the completion of his work without any gaps. Will's response is in unequivocal language implying criticism of Casaubon 'living in a lumber-room and furbishing up broken-legged theories about Chus and Mizraim'. He counters Dorothea's anger by saying that he means to be independent in the future. Dorothea responds generously, and ultimately both of them are aware of feelings – in Will's case of love, in Dorothea's of affectionate liking. Dorothea, from the best intentions, reveals Will's plans to her husband. It leads to a cold exchange which she could not have anticipated; she cannot see Casaubon's small centre of self and the jealousy it gives rise to.

BOOK III   WAITING FOR DEATH

Summary

Fred, as we have seen, has got Mr Garth to put his name to a bill for £160. He buys a new horse. This turns out to be vicious, and Fred finds that he cannot meet his debt to Caleb Garth, who has not told his wife what he has done. Fred goes on to Stone Court to confess to Mary. Angry at first, she later responds warmly to him and, later still, gives the money she has saved to her father. Fred is taken ill, and Lydgate succeeds Wrench as the Vincys' medical attendant. This places him much in Rosamond's company, but no word is said, and he continues to care for Fred. Meanwhile the Casaubons return from their honeymoon to find that Celia is engaged to Sir James Chettam. Casaubon receives a letter from Will suggesting a visit, with one enclosed for Dorothea, but is taken ill, and Lydgate is called in. Mr Brooke invites Ladislaw to Tipton, Mrs Bulstrode interrogates Rosamond about Lydgate, and the latter, after staying away, succumbs to Rosamond's appeal and finds himself engaged to her. Meanwhile the relations wait for Peter Featherstone to die, and he confides to Mary that he has made two wills, one of which he wishes to burn. Mary refuses to touch the document, and refuses to be bribed as well. Old Featherstone dies without having his last wish gratified.

Commentary

Chapter 23

The first thing to note is the wide-ranging association of the Book title *Waiting for Death*. It links the stories of Casaubon and Peter Featherstone, a stress-mark of structure, but also reaches forward to, for example, the death of Raffles which links the Bulstrode–Lydgate stories. But the immediate concern of this chapter is to describe the moral obloquy of Fred in gambling, since his debts involve the Garth family, who are industrious, hard-working people of integrity and obviously embody George Eliot's ideal, the work-ethic of responsibility. Caleb is revealed as a kindly but, where money is concerned, an impractical man. George Eliot also uses the opportunity to indicate the class difference between the Garths and the Vincys which is present in the minds of the latter, hence their fear that Fred will marry Mary. Caleb himself is a fine study in mildness and tolerance, and there is no doubt that his standards – and those of Mary and Mrs Garth – are the standards the author wishes would be observed in life.

In fact there are some omniscient touches which show George Eliot's awareness of social differences and attendant moral judgements:

> ... when a youthful nobleman steals jewellery we call the act kleptomania, speak of it with a philosophical smile, and never think of his being sent to the house of correction as if he were a ragged boy who had stolen turnips.

The whole sordid business of horse-dealing, with pleasure set in dinginess, is given a mordantly ironic flavour. Horrocks and Bambridge are caricatures, their main traits of dishonesty and unscrupulousness, with the essential accompaniment of lying, being vividly if passingly drawn. Fred is revealed as foolish and, in transaction with these men, proven sharpers, he is also shown to be naïve.

Chapter 24

A brilliant parallel is drawn succinctly when Fred's purchase turns out to be vicious – 'There was no more redress for this than the discovery of bad temper after marriage' – a relevant comment since marriages and their discordance are at the centre of *Middlemarch*. There is a sympathetic description of Mrs Garth, a tolerant, giving and caring woman without the cloying goodness that is free from fault. Again we note the moral emphasis on the work theme, but she is a genuine character who 'sustained her oddities, as a very fine wine sustains a flavour of skin'. As Fred comes to confess she is seen in typical fashion doing more than one thing at the same time. It is a natural interior, the children as convincing as their mother, and this naturalness, essentially good and unself-seeking, heightens the poignancy of Fred's position.

There is a fine irony as Mrs Garth, unaware of Fred's troubles, reveals her financial struggles on behalf of her children. It is greatly to Fred's credit, and we warm to him despite his culpability, that he speaks straight out about the loss of the money. The absence of recrimination from husband and wife makes 'Fred feel for the first time something like the tooth of remorse.' The genuine love between Caleb and his wife is movingly, naturally conveyed after Fred's departure, though Caleb, despite his lack of business acumen, has insight into Mary's feelings for Fred which his wife does not – at this stage – possess. Caleb's mention of business calls forth an authorial analogy, for he speaks of it in 'the peculiar tone of fervid veneration, of religious regard, in which he wrapped it, as a consecrated symbol is wrapped in its gold-fringed linen'.

Chapter 25
Fred's confession to Mary is natural, moving, the index to their emotions conveyed with unforced sympathetic insight. Mary's devotion to her own family, and the suffering she feels on their account, moving from passion to quietude, is balanced by Fred's concern for her and his own self-pity in these moments of anguish and humiliation. Mary is moved to anger again on her father's account by Fred's selfishness, but to compassion for Fred in his obvious suffering, her attitude 'maternal even in a girlish love'. Caleb's own appearance to tell Mary the news (which she already knows) brings out all the warmth and genuine love in Mary's nature, as she 'kissed him with childish kisses which he delighted in'. Mary's generosity with the little money she has forms an effective contrast to the money-grabbing relatives hanging around old Featherstone and the expectations of Fred and his family. Caleb's warmth on Mary's account forces him to say of Fred, 'He means better than he acts, perhaps.' He adds a more telling truth in the context of the novel, observing with quiet wisdom, 'a woman, let her be as good as she may, has got to put up with the life her husband makes for her'. We think immediately of Dorothea, but Caleb is, delicately, subduedly, blaming himself for putting his name to Fred's bill and thinking of his wife's suffering. It is a genuine expression of love. Mary's own acknowledged love for Fred, with its firm moral basis and insistence on his becoming responsible, reassures Caleb. We note too old Featherstone's insight into the reasons for Caleb's visit.

Chapter 26
Fred's illness finds Mr Wrench wanting – 'Great statesmen, and why not small medical men?' – observes the author laconically, and this gives Rosamond the opportunity, without being devious, to get Lydgate into the house, and 'to show a pretty anxiety conflicting with her sense of what was becoming'. Mrs Vincy's reaction is irrationally directed against Wrench, Mr Vincy's even more bluntly so, and Lydgate realises that 'To be puffed by ignorance was not only humiliating, but perilous.' None the less he accepts the case, and what George Eliot earlier called 'the stealthy convergence of human lots' is now drawing him and Rosamond into closer proximity. There is a finely satirical account of current gossip, one Mrs Taft believing that 'Lydgate was a natural son of Bulstrode's', which not only

underlines the facility of gossip, but also has resonance in the forthcoming arrival of another natural son, Joshua Rigg Featherstone. As Mrs Farebrother observes, in the consummate close to the chapter, 'the report may be true of some other son'.

Chapter 27

This chapter opens with the image of the pier-glass as parable, with the scratches as 'events' and 'the candle is the egoism of any person now absent – of Miss Vincy, for example'. The image in fact defines George Eliot's creative method, with the illumination the focus on character, and the scratches the interrelatedness of her characters' lives, one of the major unifying strands in *Middlemarch*. This is followed by an account of Mrs Vincy's suffering, which has something of a comic element in it – 'she was like a sick bird with languid eye and plumage ruffled' – but it is also moving in her dependence on Lydgate. His constant visits provide Rosamond with the opportunity to be seen to advantage, and there is a bonus to the illness, almost offsetting worry, when Peter Featherstone makes it known that he needs Fred. The latter, drained by his illness, thinks much of Mary, while Lydgate, fascinated by Rosamond, begins 'calling himself her captive – meaning, all the while, not to be her captive'. As for Rosamond, 'She seemed to be sailing with a fair wind just whither she would go', another of the unifying images in the novel.

There is a considered stress on Rosamond's small attractions and admirable sense of propriety throughout, but certainly Lydgate is 'the doomed man of that date', his own perspective on their relationship being that it is merely flirtation. The superiority of Lydgate is demonstrated in the discussion of the 'Keepsake', his satirical remarks about the engravings and the writers driving off young Plymdale (though we are told that Rosamond 'liked to excite jealousy'). The bear and the bird analogy – which Rosamond undoubtedly thinks of as the private language of their love – helps to convince her that 'she and Lydgate were as good as engaged'. Lydgate himself at this stage is still enjoying his experiments, enjoying too the prospect of a feud with the other medical men and enjoying the tastes of success – he is called in to attend Casaubon.

Chapter 28

The ironic motto to the chapter is reinforced by some fine atmospheric writing as Dorothea, glowing with life, enters the room where everything seems to have shrunk, 'the stag in the tapestry looked more like a ghost' being a symbolic stroke to emphasise the diminishing of her own life. She feels a strange companionship with the miniature of Will's grandmother, perhaps a subconscious association that Will may ultimately be the means of freeing her from this 'moral imprisonment', though of course she cannot be aware of this. It is a subtle notation on George Eliot's part. Dorothea's next reaction is one of guilt for what she has said to her husband. But she is silently warm to Celia, Mr Brooke tells her that 'Rome has agreed' with her, and Dorothea, questioned by Celia, begins her concealment about her honeymoon. Celia's news, that she is engaged to Sir James, outweighs all else, Dorothea responding cautiously (conditioned by her own marriage experiences) then warmly to her sister who regards 'Mr Casaubon's learning as a kind of damp which might in due time saturate a neighbouring body'. We note the image and the half-conscious insight of Celia.

Chapter 29

A deft narrative balance is struck here by a switch to Casaubon's consciousness, which is 'intense'. Casaubon's sexual impotence is analogous to his scholarly failure. His views – that his wife would be 'submissive', 'educable', a 'helpmate' and would 'think her husband's mind powerful' – would today be called chauvinistic, but despite his 'narrow sensitiveness' he has scruples and is a 'man of honour'. His rooted insecurity, particularly about what is thought by other scholars of his work, means that he never escapes 'from a small hungry shivering self'. We note the irony in the names chosen for his critical contemporaries – Carp, Pike, Tench – living predatory fish as distinct from the manuscript fish deities which occupy some of his attention. He is driven even more in upon himself by Will's letter suggesting he pay them a visit – and of course by his unvoiced jealousy of Will's letter to Dorothea. The latter tells an unpleasant truth when she accuses Casaubon of speaking 'as if I were something you had to contend against'. There is a moving contrast between Casaubon's trembling hand and Dorothea's firm one, but Dorothea finds 'her whole soul melted into tender alarm' when she finds Casaubon 'in some bodily distress'. While Lydgate, conveniently near ('and giving his arm to Miss Vincy') is on his way, Sir James reiterates the 'sacrifice' of Dorothea, but when he sees her with her arm round her husband's neck, 'He did not know how much penitence there was in the sorrow.'

Chapter 30

There is a quiet indication that Lydgate is in advance of his time through his use of the stethoscope (George Eliot's research is inevitably meticulous) on Casaubon, and Mr Brooke contributes his usual irrelevance by suggesting that Casaubon goes fishing and has Dorothea read authors who are a 'little broad' to him, like Smollett. Fittingly, Lydgate speaks to Dorothea in the 'sombre light' of the library, and is deeply touched by Dorothea's emotional response, though the author observes, 'Women just like Dorothea had not entered into his traditions.' Nevertheless he remembers her appeal – 'this cry from soul to soul' – and when he has gone she reads the letters, realising that she must prevent Will from coming to Lowick. By an unfortunate error of judgement she gets Mr Brooke to deal with this; Mr Brooke's pen – and his mind – run away with the idea of getting Ladislaw to Tipton in order to run his newly acquired newspaper the 'Middlemarch Pioneer'. His invitation carries long-term effects unknown to him, for Casaubon is to suspect Will and Dorothea as a result of this ill-considered action of her uncle's.

Chapter 31

The 'stealthy convergence of human lots' now operates to Rosamond's advantage, though not without some suffering to that young lady. Mrs Bulstrode, with Fred and Mrs Vincy at Stone Court (propitiating Peter Featherstone and keeping watch on Mary Garth respectively) determines to speak to Rosamond in order to find out if she is engaged to Lydgate. There is a fine ironic play as each woman surveys the other's fashionable dress. Rosamond is embarrassed, and Bulstrode later confirms to his wife that Lydgate has no intention of getting married. A fine sense of anticipation is built up in the narrative. Mrs Bulstrode's emotional pressure on Lydgate is consummately if inquisitively done, while Mr Farebrother's casual implication that he and Lydgate will meet at the Vincys that evening gives the young idealist food for thought. Ironically he thinks that Rosamond would not have misunderstood his intentions (we know that she has) and determines to stay away; Rosamond feels the lack of his company as keenly as possible or, as the author puts it, 'as a charming stage Ariadne left behind with all her boxes full of costumes and no hope of a coach'. By one of those chances which change the direction of lives, Lydgate determines to call (with news of Peter Featherstone's deterioration) on Mrs Vincy, deluding himself that he can treat Rosamond lightly. His retrieval of the chain, the flower/water imagery which accompanies his recognition of her distress, his tenderness, the quick transition to his being 'an engaged man', are managed with high narrative art, carrying as it does the irony of delusion, of succumbing to temptation, of the lack of real knowledge each has of the other. The word 'demise' in relation to Peter Featherstone has 'seasonably' occurred to Mr Vincy; it aptly fits Lydgate, since it is the beginning of his.

Chapter 32

This is central to the Book title, since it evokes the internecine family resentment as the relations wait for Peter Featherstone to die. Their expectations are given with humorous facility, often in appropriately witty language ('an own brother "lying there" with dropsy in his legs must come to feel that blood was thicker than water'). There is an ironic anticipation of the scene to come later in the reference to 'forged wills and disputed wills', and a dramatic and claustrophobic feeling wonderfully conveyed 'that everybody must watch over everybody else'. The invidious position of Mary Garth is stressed; she has to endure the wit of the swindler Jonah, who is very suspicious of her, and the idiocy of young Cranch, who sometimes reduces her to laughter. Featherstone remains immune: 'Too languid to sting, he had the more venom refluent in his blood.' His driving of his relatives from the bedroom door has a touch of grotesque dark comedy about it.

There is the finely drawn portrait, somewhat Dickensian in flavour, of Featherstone's second cousin, the auctioneer who has 'nothing more than a sincere sense of his own merit'. Mr Borthrop Trumbull comes in for his due share of authorial irony, for this 'amateur of superior phrases' is always correcting himself. His handling of the relatives, each intent upon finding out what they can about old Featherstone's intentions, is a masterly display of self-importance, since he knows nothing about Peter Featherstone's will. He is an inveterate collector of books valued by their outsides and of paintings for display without understanding.

Chapter 33

The motto is chosen as ironically illustrative of Peter Featherstone's death. This is one of the most dramatic scenes in the novel, filled with the might-have-been (for Fred Vincy) if Mary had not been a girl of integrity. Her common-sense thoughts and natural intuition give her a closely reasoned feeling that Fred will be disappointed. Then Peter Featherstone rouses into directness. Used to rule in life, he is thwarted on the eve of death by Mary's steadfast refusal to interfere with the two wills he has made. It is a scene of striking emphasis, the author's moral stance enfolding Mary and the rightness of her decision. Admittedly Mary's language is a little strained though truthful – 'I will not let the close of your life soil the beginning of mine.' Bribery fails, yet there is still an encompassing pathos as she saw 'old Peter Featherstone begin to cry childishly'. His death after impotently throwing the stick at her, the atmosphere of the room and the tensions of Mary's consciousness, show George Eliot at her best, graphic, dramatic, poignant, psychologically true, the tight folds of style perfectly conveying the realism of Mary's experience and the thwarting of the wicked old man. Finally there is the irony of the effects of her actions, not least on the man she loves and who loves her.

BOOK IV   THREE LOVE PROBLEMS

Summary

First there is the burial of Peter Featherstone. The funeral procession, watched by Dorothea and Celia, includes the legatees as well as Lydgate and Vincy, so that all the main characters of the novel are present. Will is also there by Mr Brooke's invitation. The wills are read, Fred benefiting handsomely from the first, which is superseded by the second in favour of one Joshua Rigg. Mr Vincy's reaction – severity to Fred and a threat to Rosamond's engagement – in fact hastens the marriage of Rosamond and Lydgate.

The broad reform background is given as Will edits the 'Pioneer' for that potential 'reform' candidate, Mr Brooke; he also finds time to visit Lowick and sees Dorothea. Casaubon writes to him forbidding him to come to the house, and Dorothea, unaware, angers her husband by urging him to do more for Will. Sir James and the Cadwalladers discuss Mr Brooke's impropriety. Dorothea learns that Will has been forbidden the house, and Mr Brooke, whose own farms require reform, is berated by one of his tenants, Dagley. Mr Garth is invited to manage the Chettam estates and those of Mr Brooke; he also thinks of inviting Fred to help him. Joshua Rigg takes Stone Court, and gets rid of a disreputable companion from his past, John Raffles. Meanwhile Casaubon broods that, if he dies, Will may marry Dorothea, and asks Lydgate to tell him the truth about his condition. Lydgate does, Casaubon is cold to Dorothea but she waits up for him, and he speaks kindly to her.

Commentary

Chapter 34
Featherstone's hand, like Casaubon's later, reaches beyond the grave; the author's humour plays over the mourners who have been summoned to attend and the observers who comment on them. 'The country gentry of old time lived in a rarefied air', but there is some integration of them into Middlemarch as a whole when they witness this 'odd funeral'. There is plenty of social comment, but the dramatic stroke is the revelation of Ladislaw's presence and its effect on Dorothea, as well as the 'sort of frog-face' pungently observed by Mrs Cadwallader. The loneliness of Casaubon, the distance between him and Dorothea, is emphasised by the fact that he believes that Dorothea is responsible for Will being invited to the Grange. Thus their misunderstandings continue, though Dorothea's sensitivity tells her that Mr Brooke's ramblings in praise of the unwelcome Ladislaw are 'about as pleasant as a grain of sand in the eye of Mr Casaubon'.

Chapter 35
Meanwhile the 'Christian Carnivora' gather in jealous expectation and fear to hear the reading of the will. There is dramatic and apprehensive speculation about the identity of the stranger, while Mrs Waule and Mrs Cranch assume a kind of choric function. Mr Vincy, surveying the gathering, feels some optimism and Fred, also optimistic, some humour at the thought of the stranger being a 'love-child'. There is more humour in the fact that a considerable lawyer like Mr Standish has been fooled by old Featherstone, and the meticulous dating contributes to the tension present. The reactions of the various relations badly treated by Featherstone are comments on that natural human failing, greed, and Fred's initial triumph is squashed with the reading of the second will which, we remember, the old man wished to destroy. Mary's sense of her own involvement in the finality leads her to speak warmly to Fred, who reacts 'pettishly'. The final authorial comment in the chapter marks the much broader tide of history, for Peter Featherstone 'was dead and buried some months before Lord Grey came into office'. It brings political and moral perspective to the petty ambitions which we have just witnessed, with Mary and Caleb the only characters who emerge morally unscarred.

Chapter 36
This describes the Vincy interaction, again with an emphasis on the might-have-been in Fred's reactions to his dream of a comfortable hunting life –

and perhaps winning Mary – shattered. Mrs Vincy has the capacity at once to soothe her husband over Fred and then stir him up about Rosamond's engagement. Vincy tends to speak in extremes – natural in the heat of the moment – and then back down, though he employs his wife here to tell Rosamond. The latter displays 'perfect obstinacy' and, as Mrs Vincy foresees, manages her father, who 'had as little of his own way as if he had been a prime minister', another ironic linking of the small world with the large.

Again, natural images – of the rock, of frost, of day – are used, as well as the unifying image of the web to define the courtship of Rosamond and Lydgate. Rosamond is said to be 'in the water-lily's expanding wonderment at its own fuller life'. The web is 'mutual', the ironic emphasis being that it is a trap. Mrs Bulstrode busies herself in Rosamond's affairs again, consults her husband, feeling that he 'was one of those men whose memoirs should be written when they died'. The irony is that events are to prove her wrong. Lydgate meanwhile believes that things will always be as they are in his 'personal pride and unreflecting egoism', and that marriage will enable him to work more steadily. He is also snobbish towards the Vincys. His love for Rosamond is based on strong physical attraction and a complete lack of knowledge of what is going on in her mind – there is a like lack of knowledge about Lydgate in hers. Her eyes are on Quallingham and the supposedly aristocratic connections she is set on cultivating.

Chapter 37
The political emphasis in small (Middlemarch) and large (the era of the Reform Bill) is given a considered stress now that Mr Brooke is known to have bought the 'Pioneer'. The discussion of this is spicy, particularly from Mr Hawley, who, having called Mr Brooke 'a stray tortoise', prophesies that Ladislaw will 'begin with flourishing about the Rights of Man and end with murdering a wench'. Mr Brooke, whose own farms are in need of reform, misguidedly feels that he can put Ladislaw on the 'right tack' while that 'winter-worn husband' Casaubon resents Will's presence in the area anyway. Will continues to react in hyperbolical terms to the marriage of Dorothea and Casaubon, thinking it 'the most horrible of virgin-sacrifices'. He will devote himself to her, but we note that his 'passionate prodigality' is not psychologically integrated, and that there is some failure on George Eliot's part to make him convincing.

Dorothea welcomes Will's company, the now familiar imagery categorising her reactions as 'a lunette opened in the wall of her prison, giving her a glimpse of the sunny air'. A delicious authorial irony draws a parallel with Dante and Beatrice, Petrarch and Laura as Will contrives to see Dorothea. When he does, her response is one of 'simple sincerity'. They are compared to 'two flowers which had opened then and there', while Dorothea feels as if there is 'fresh water at her thirsty lips to speak without fear'. She reveals to Will her deep-rooted need to serve someone 'who did great works'. Will's hyperbolical reactions continue and he thinks of 'beautiful lips kissing holy skulls and other emptinesses ecclesiastically enshrined'. The imagery continues to distance him from reality. But he moves Dorothea more deeply than he is aware of, and reveals details of his early life of suffering which calls forth her sympathy and idealism. She also makes excuses for her husband, though not in any disloyal way. Will, intent on her approval, persuades her to say that she hopes he will stay in the area, thus unconsciously ensuring further friction between her and Casaubon, though Dorothea tells him that her husband should be the judge of whether he should stay or not.

Will hastens his departure, not wishing to become 'ray-shorn in her eyes'. Dorothea has a naïve capacity for putting her foot in it, and does so when she reveals Will's occupation to Casaubon. The latter's letter to Will is a masterpiece of pedantic self-righteousness; Dorothea, unaware, enjoys in a somewhat muted way the mute companionship of stag and miniatures in her boudoir. She is determined to have more money given to Ladislaw to help him towards a positive occupation, but her 'blindness' causes her to blunder again by suggesting this to Casaubon. He is jealously quick to believe that Will has initiated this, and puts her interference down with a chill finality. There follows Will's letter asserting his right to independent action which Casaubon – not without some cause – attributes to his wish to subvert Dorothea from him. The chapter ends on a note of ominous disharmony to come, with Casaubon 'mentally preparing other measures of frustration'.

Chapter 38

Mr Brooke's actions are discussed by Sir James and the Cadwalladers, the local political scene now coming to the foreground, with Mr Brooke having the support of Bulstrode. Mrs Cadwallader considers that he will 'make a splash in the mud', and her tongue embraces 'that dangerous young sprig' Ladislaw. Interestingly, the Rector thinks that Ladislaw and Mr Brooke will tire of one another, while his wife rightly points out that Mr Brooke will not enjoy spending money on an election. The campaign against Mr Brooke as a non-reforming landlord is foreshadowed. We note that both Sir James and Cadwallader are intent on advancing Caleb Garth – the recognition of his worth is a measure of their integrity – and with the appearance of Mr Brooke Mrs Cadwallader looks forward to a little baiting. Cadwallader himself begins it by a telling quotation from that rival organ the 'Trumpet' on Mr Brooke's meanness. His reaction, and the emphasis on bribery, as well as the anticipation of Mr Brooke being pelted (which he later is) is delightfully ironic humour, the Cadwalladers and their zest for life neatly balancing the genuine anger and concern of Sir James Chettam on Mr Brooke's account.

Chapter 39

Will's response to Dorothea's arrival at the Grange (her 'entrance was the freshness of morning') shows how deeply in love he is, for he is 'ridiculously disappointed' when she appears too self-absorbed to notice him. Dorothea, 'with characteristic directness', tells her uncle that she has heard he intends to improve his farms, but Brooke, equally characteristically, temporises. Dorothea continues to cite chapter and verse about her experiences of the poverty on his farms (ironically mentioning Dagley, with whom Mr Brooke is shortly to tangle). Will sees 'a certain greatness in her' and is somewhat chastened. She is 'much moved' when she learns that Will has been forbidden to come to Lowick. The exchange between them is redolent of his ardent love and her innocent warmth of response.

Her own idealism is couched in the imagery we have come to associate with her life experience – 'we are part of the divine power against evil – widening the skirts of light and making the struggle with darkness narrower'. An authorial image somehow lessens the effect – 'They were looking at each other like two fond children who were talking confidentially of birds.' There follows the drive to Dagley's (with Mr Brooke's wonderfully inconsequential tale of the Methodist preacher who killed a hare), with a detailed description of this rather run-down farm and its 'pauper labourers'. Dagley, having had too much to drink and 'too much in the shape of muddy political talk', is bent on countering Mr Brooke's condescension with an aggressive rebelliousness, and the result is one of the best scenes of *Middlemarch*, with its truth to the time, to the sordid reality of farming conditions, and to the difference of social classes here shown. The dialect and moods of Dagley and his wife are equally convincing, the bitterness in Dagley consonant with the talk of 'Rinform' and Mr Brooke's ambiguous association with it.

Chapter 40

This chapter opens with a scientific analogy – the electric battery – in order to bring about a change of perspective, here a switch to the Garth family. Mary typically is working at a handkerchief for Rosamond – the work-ethic in miniature, so to speak – and the family scene is a touching one. It is all immediately and movingly offset by Mr Garth's good news about the Freshitt and Tipton offers, almost as if goodness and decency have triumphed despite the ways of the world. Caleb interestingly has his own ideas for reforming the Brooke estate – even more interestingly, they bear comparison with Dorothea's – and Caleb's inherent generosity transfers itself to thinking that he may be able to do something for Fred. The latter has sent Mr Farebrother to make his goodbyes to the Garths, an indication of his deep sense of compunction over being unable to pay the money. We note too Mr Farebrother's goodness and his fondness for Mary, even deference to her, but when Caleb tells Farebrother the story of Mary's refusal to destroy the will that would have made Fred old Featherstone's heir, Farebrother is now aware of that moral dilemma. There is a strong focus on the essential goodness and ordinariness of Mary.

The author's perspective leaves us to decide whether Mary prefers Farebrother to Fred, the one she respects before the one she would like to respect. Mrs Garth's common sense is employed to show her husband that if he offers Fred work – which the Vincys will consider beneath him – they will also consider that he is doing it in order to ensure that Fred marries Mary. Caleb, in his honesty of intention, is disgusted at this. In terms of the plot, the chapter ends with the interesting competition of Bulstrode and Joshua Rigg for Stone Court.

Chapter 41
After a 'lofty comparison' there is a considered description of Joshua Rigg, with his cool and calculating nature, a nice touch which gives him a filial consistency with old Featherstone. He is seen in contrast with the florid and disreputable Raffles, married to Joshua's mother and an inveterate sponger. Again the money theme is evident, but both men appear to be caricatures rather than the flesh and blood creations we have been responding to in *Middlemarch*. This chapter furthers the plot, because the paper which Raffles picks up is signed by Bulstrode, but there is also a neat historical placing – the coming of change – since he travels on 'the new-made railway'.

Chapter 42
The main strand of the plot involves Casaubon brooding on his unacknowledged failure, his sad and jealously-guarded present, and a determination to further guard the future possessively if he dies. The complexity of Casaubon's suffering with regard to Dorothea is finely conveyed. He feels a degree of guilt, but mainly he is suspicious of Ladislaw's intentions and Dorothea's unawareness of them. Again the image of the web is used, for his 'suspicion and jealousy . . . were constantly at their weaving work', while the image associated with Casaubon – 'carrying his taper among the tombs of the past' – is evocative of his failure in the present. There is a fine investigation of his motives, given in the form of a monologue before Casaubon sees Lydgate. Though we may dislike the strength of his jealous bias against Will, we cannot help feeling the essential loneliness and deprivation of the man.

The contrast with Lydgate is given a considered emphasis, while the beauty of the afternoon where 'the lights and shadows slept side by side' is symbolic of the contrast between vibrant life and approaching death, between the practical idealism of Lydgate and the intellectual aridity of Casaubon. His mode of address to Lydgate is almost a parody of his habitual style, so much so that Lydgate 'felt a little amusement mingling with his pity'. His truthful and direct statement to Casaubon is followed by our deepening awareness of Casaubon's inner state as he sees the nearness of death. Dorothea's gesture of sympathy is rebuffed as he 'allowed her pliant arm to cling with difficulty against his rigid arm'. He shuts himself away, Dorothea passes through anguish to anger – 'In such a crisis as this, some women begin to hate' – and then to lonely meditation and a kind of humility, which ends with her waiting in the darkness for Casaubon to come to bed. In one of those wonderful transitions, one of those moments when human nature is laid bare, Casaubon is moved to kindness by her waiting for him, and we are moved by the quality of compassion and understanding that brings this incompatible pair hand in hand 'along the broad corridor together'.

BOOK V THE DEAD HAND

Summary

Dorothea calls on Lydgate and meets Rosamond (now Mrs Lydgate) and Will. She later goes to the New Hospital to see Lydgate, and tells her husband that she intends to subscribe two hundred a year to it. Middlemarch gossip that Lydgate was not dispensing drugs gives way to his fortuitously successful treatment of patients and, in the case of Borthrop Trumbull, his expertise. Opposed by the other practitioners over the fever hospital, Lydgate finds also the beginnings of opposition in Rosamond. The wider political reform makes itself felt in Middlemarch. Will Ladislaw is dissatisfied with his role as Mr Brooke's hireling; he sees Dorothea at church, but is cut by Mr Casaubon, who later becomes wakeful and alert.

Dorothea, asked to carry out Casaubon's wishes with respect to continuing his work on mythology, begs for time to consider; she goes to give Casaubon her answer and finds him dead. His will disinherits her of the property *if* she marries Ladislaw. Dorothea is deeply hurt. Later, Lydgate presses upon her the claims of Farebrother to the vacant living. Mr Brooke makes a disastrous speech which effectively negates his candidature, and gives up the 'Pioneer', though Will decides to continue to live in Middlemarch. Farebrother gets the Lowick living, Fred takes his degree, and Mary remains staunch in her views that Fred should not become a clergyman. At the same time, with Farebrother on the edge of proposing to her, she refuses to give up Fred. Bulstrode buys Stone Court from Joshua Rigg; Raffles turns up and accosts Bulstrode, whom he says he knew twenty-five years ago. Raffles stays the night at Stone Court, obviously intent on getting what he can out of Bulstrode. The latter's guilty past has caught up with him, and Raffles obtains £200 from him and leaves.

Commentary

Chapter 43

Dorothea's visit to Lowick Gate provides the reader and Will with a chance to note the contrast between the two women, the essential simplicity and candour of Dorothea and the 'infantine blondness' and 'that controlled self-consciousness of manner which is the expensive substitute for simplicity' of Rosamond. The effect on Dorothea of seeing Will is immediate and mixed; she wonders at Will's being alone with Rosamond (though he has at times been alone with her too). Her susceptibility – her unacknowledged love for Will – moves her to tears, but her natural resilience asserts itself once she is with Lydgate at the hospital. Will's reaction is typically impetuous and he is sulky with Rosamond, who rides his petulant worship of Dorothea very well. She sees at once the situation, but when Lydgate returns the dialogue between husband and wife, warm on his part and moderately responsive on hers, gives hints of the distance there is to be between them.

Chapter 44

This brief chapter has a tellingly unifying and brief motto as the two idealists Lydgate and Dorothea meet. It reflects openness and courage, the poignancy coming from the fact that Dorothea's 'mid-sea' idealism has been muted by her marriage, whereas Lydgate at this time is following 'the guidance of the stars', developing his ideas in the New Hospital. Dorothea, characteristically forgetful of self when others' needs are put to her, responds generously from the heart and later from the pocket. Lydgate is seen at his best, pursuing his career yet without a salary for the hospital work. The chapter ends on a sad note, with Casaubon aware that Dorothea has spoken to Lydgate about him, but 'He distrusted her affection; and what loneliness is more lonely than distrust?'

Chapter 45

Bulstrode's attitudes towards opposition are called 'the ministerial views', an image used earlier to describe him in relation to Lydgate. We note that George Eliot embraces a spectrum of Middlemarch views on Lydgate and the hospital, and captures the gossips' distortion by spicing it with a contemporary reference to the body-snatchers, Burke and Hare. Lydgate reveals his capacity for indiscretion in talking to Mr Mawmsey (it is one of his spots of commonness), for human nature being what it is people have come to rely upon mixtures or drugs, feeling that they must be getting something for their money. The tone throughout is satirical, ironic, with the various reactions of the medical men tending to throw discredit on Lydgate's integrity, a neatly turned moral point, since Lydgate in his profession acts throughout from the best motives. Lydgate, however, profits from 'fortune's testimonials', and receives 'that ignorant praise which misses every valid quality'. His treatment of Trumbull shows his acute psychological penetration, as he knows just how to propitiate the pompous auctioneer in order to practise his waiting and watching theory.

The Fever Hospital, with Lydgate having absolute authority in the medical treatment, removes him from the Middlemarch practitioners completely. It also ensures that Lydgate will devote more and more time to this financially unprofitable work, thus contributing to his ultimate domestic crisis. Even here there is some humour, as the unctuous Bulstrode claims the support of Mr Brooke, though 'he has not specified a sum – probably not a great one'. Farebrother shows his friendship, qualified by good advice to Lydgate, to separate himself from Bulstrode as much as possible and to avoid getting into financial difficulties. Lydgate has the 'fulness of contemplative thought', but when he tells Rosamond of his work and ideals the distance between them is obvious. She is appalled by the story of Vesalius having to get bodies for his research from the gallows, but a brilliant authorial linking has Lydgate tell the story of how he 'died rather miserably', an exact and unconscious forecast of what is to happen to him. Rosamond's distaste for his profession, her not knowing the real man, is carried off here by her coquettish humour, but Lydgate ends by 'giving up remonstrance and petting her resignedly'. It is the future story of their life together.

Chapter 46

References to Lord John Russell and Grey (see chapter 3 of this study) give the wider political perspective which has its local political equivalent in the activities of Ladislaw and the 'Pioneer', ironically ineffectual because of the vacillations of Mr Brooke. Will is a positive radical, and there is even a forecast of his own future career in Parliament which is sketched in the Finale. Though his work is not 'the loftiest thing', he goes into it, as Mr Brooke would say, thoroughly, and even takes fire from it. He thinks of himself as an Under-Secretary – 'the little waves make the large ones and are of the same pattern' – and George Eliot takes a proprietory delight in presenting him as being of no class or caste.

Gossip about Lydgate is balanced by gossip about Mr Brooke taking up Ladislaw. The latter is given a considered set of eccentricities – fluent speaking on political platforms, entertaining groups of ragged children, stretching himself out on rugs when he visits other people – which are meant to be endearing but do not stand up to the cold light of criticism or reality. Lydgate is clear-sighted about politics and reform, Will engagingly opportunist. Lydgate typically uses medical analogies to declare his political view. The overall parallel is between Mr Brooke and Bulstrode, men who are fallible but are on the side of right even if their motivations are wrong. Lydgate advocates a man's 'personal independence' free from 'private interest' and the argument with Ladislaw again shows Will's fiery nature – he interprets this to mean that he has lost his independence by working for Brooke and having expectations from him.

Chapter 47

Ladislaw broods after his exchange with Lydgate, restless and dissatisfied with himself for the course of action he has taken. His idealisation of Dorothea has her for ever 'enthroned in his soul'. He thinks in the hyperbole common to him, 'stay he would, whatever fire-breathing dragons might hiss around her'. Objection and Inclination personified fight out his wish to see her, and when he sets out the familiar imagery describes his smile as being as 'pleasant to see as the breaking of sunshine on the water'. But this 'bright creature, abundant in uncertain promises' feeds his 'frugal cheer' with a poor lyric which was 'not exactly a hymn'. His sufferings, his realisation that he has been wrong to come to the church to see Dorothea, are movingly conveyed, but we are made aware of Dorothea's sufferings too 'as if she were suppressing tears'.

Chapter 48

Dorothea, intent on believing that Will's presence carried a hope of reconciliation, is now 'robbed of that hope'. There is some fine atmospheric writing which is consonant with Dorothea's mood and her situation. She is living in a 'tomb' and is denied the 'light', while the 'spring flowers and the grass had a dull shiver in them'. Later Casaubon displays a remarkable quickness in surveying his work and, in the night, Dorothea is woken by 'a sense of light, which seemed to her at first like a sudden vision of sunset after she had climbed a steep hill', a telling symbolic equivalent of her wish for 'light', the climb being the burden of her present life. The 'bird-like speed' of Casaubon's mind leaves Dorothea 'sick at heart', but his trying to exact a promise from her to do what he wishes her to do finds Dorothea resistant. She knows from experience – and here she is clear-sighted – that 'sifting those mixed heaps of material' would be futile. After her anguished night of arguing to and fro – structurally equivalent to Will's Objection and Inclination inward debate – Dorothea still delays. Casaubon's death comes as a masterly dramatic – and poignant – stroke at the end of the chapter.

Chapter 49
Another brief chapter which exemplifies the Book title, for this second dead hand ensures that Dorothea will lose her property if she marries Will, and thus Casaubon's insecurity and jealousy are perpetuated beyond the grave. Sir James, in his altercation with Mr Brooke, reveals that he is warmly protective to Dorothea, indeed we suspect that he is still half in love with her. Mr Brooke, ineffectual on this level, is bound to be ineffectual in political life, and he uses the worst possible term as far as Sir James is concerned by calling Ladislaw 'an agitator'.

Chapter 50
Celia is absorbed in her baby, but sharp and pert enough to think Dorothea fortunate in having lost a husband who had 'been so dull and troublesome while he lived'. Outside Dorothea's small world the large world exists, the imminent dissolution of Parliament paralleling her imminent discovery of the provisions of the will. Dorothea with typical practicality and independence decides to make her own decision about who shall have her husband's living. Despite the baby, Dorothea becomes self-absorbed, and Celia, armed with her usual bluntness and with 'persevering quietude' tells Dorothea of the codicil to the will. Celia has timed the revelation perfectly, but Dorothea experiences revulsion towards her dead husband and a 'sudden strange yearning of heart towards Will Ladislaw'. With the appearance of Lydgate she sobs, but he is enlightened enough to see that she needs 'perfect freedom . . . more than any other prescription'.

Going through her husband's papers she recalls her unvoiced promise, but this is now influenced by her awareness of Casaubon's 'hidden alienation of secrecy and suspicion'. With that spring of resilience which we have previously noted, Dorothea turns towards duty and the question of the living. Lydgate, remembering his own convenient vote for Tyke in the past, warmly recommends Farebrother for the vacancy. Dorothea has already looked at a volume of Tyke's sermons and found them unsuitable for Lowick, but Lydgate mentions Ladislaw and, when he has gone, Dorothea finds herself thinking of Mrs Cadwallader's description of Will as 'An Italian with white mice.' She is moved by the injustice of it, for her own certainty is that 'he was a creature who entered into every one's feelings'.

Chapter 51

Ladislaw is divided between his work and thoughts of Dorothea, but irritated now that he is being kept away from the Grange by Mr Brooke, the irony being that Will, of course, does not yet know about the codicil. Imagery of 'the chasm' and 'the brink' now indicate for Will how far he is from her, but he is concerned to get Mr Brooke to pledge 'himself to vote for the actual Reform Bill'. Brooke – as usual – vacillates, his exchange with Mr Mawmsey revealing his limitations, for he ends 'with a sense of being a little out at sea, though finding it still enjoyable'. There is humour in this, but the richest humour is still to come. Mr Brooke's second glass of sherry is too much for him, and the sea imagery is employed with a tellingly ironic effect when he begins, but the scene is as much visual as verbal, a sense of atmosphere being created which is on the edge of action. We feel the excitement, but the author's commentary is laced with sarcasm as Mr Brooke 'fell back on himself and his qualifications – always an appropriate graceful subject for a candidate'. Even more appropriately he refers to *The Rambler*, a word which defines his own lack of method, and with the raising of the effigy and the 'Punch-voiced echo of his words' George Eliot cleverly exploits the effect of parody on the candidate who is himself a parody. The running humour has both wit and cruelty in it, but most effectively it conveys the truth about Mr Brooke's lack of reform on his own estates, thus demonstrating the hypocrisy of his standing as a reform candidate.

What is also being exposed is political corruption, the fact that men are employed to undertake the bringing down of a candidate – the last thing to be reformed is bribery. Meanwhile Ladislaw is communing with his own ideals and his wish to serve Dorothea. Mr. Brooke, having dug 'a channel' (note the image) is persuaded to withdraw for the good of his supporters but Ladislaw, as independent as ever, determines to stay in Middlemarch in order to be near Dorothea.

Chapter 52

The warm interior of the old-fashioned parlour when Mr Farebrother learns that he has got the Lowick living is vivid with the eccentricities of his family. There is a moving suggestion that he may now be in a position to marry, the family favourite obviously being Mary Garth; but there is retrospect on his clear and honest exchange with Dorothea and with Lydgate. Fred's confiding his own problems to him finds Mr Farebrother equal to the burden, though it is an exacting one, particularly as he himself is very fond of Mary Garth. He sacrifices himself to Fred's – and ultimately to Mary's – interests, finding appropriate language to express his position, for 'Decidedly I am an old stalk,' he thought, 'the young growths are pushing me aside.'

Mary is adept at concealing her feelings but those feelings beat strongly within her when Farebrother begins to speak of Fred. His own sense of

fairness is remarkable, and his directness over the will – the fact that the
first will would not have stood anyway if the second had been burned –
shows his unselfish concern for Mary's feelings. He is sensitive enough to
know that she might consider marrying Fred 'as an act of atonement'.
Mary's sense of principle makes her reject the idea of Fred as a clergyman,
since she would feel, and rightly, that he was 'a caricature', and she expands
upon this by saying that he must actually *do* something worthy and not
just talk about doing it. Mr Farebrother hints at his own love for Mary
with 'grave restrained emotion', and she tells him with clarity and directness that she cannot give up Fred, though she will not promise to marry
him until he proves that he is worthy.

Chapter 53
With Bulstrode having purchased Stone Court and Mr Farebrother preaching at 'the quaint little church' there, we are given some retrospect on
Joshua Rigg. As Bulstrode feels particularly serene Nemesis in the shape
of Raffles reappears from the past. Caleb witnesses their meeting but his
scruples, his moral sense, forbid him to stay. Bulstrode is visibly shaken by
the encounter, but maintains a tone of dignity and distance as the revelations threaten his peace of mind. Raffles takes delight in tormenting
Bulstrode, who, having left him at Stone Court for the night, has sensitivity
enough and morbid introspection to see himself disgraced 'in the presence
of his neighbours and of his own wife'. The next morning provides a fine
contrast, the delightful home and its outside seen against the blackmailer
within. Raffles provides plot information, the fact that Bulstrode married
an old widow, that Raffles had found her daughter and grandchild but had
been persuaded by Bulstrode not to reveal the fact, Bulstrode intending to
inherit his wife's money and business. Bulstrode's 'sickly body' is equated
with his emotional and spiritual sickness as he is told that his previous
wife's daughter may still be alive, and that she had married. Later, and this
is important to the unravelling of the plot, he remembers that her husband's
name was Ladislaw.

BOOK VI   THE WIDOW AND THE WIFE

Summary

Dorothea returns to Lowick, conscious of the fact that she wants to see
Will, who comes to say goodbye. Later Dorothea tells Celia that she will
not marry again, and consults Caleb about improvements. The railway
agents come to Frick, near Middlemarch, are resented by the farm labourers
who, in turn, are pacified by Caleb with Fred's help. Caleb determines to
take Fred on and advance his career, knowing that Mary is in love with
him. Mrs Garth reveals to Fred that Farebrother himself loves Mary, but
when Fred goes to see Mary, Farebrother delicately leaves them alone
together. Rosamond loses her baby through going out horse-riding with
Captain Lydgate, Lydgate gets into debt, Rosamond does not understand,

and disagreement grows between them. Rosamond meanwhile reveals to Ladislaw the nature of the codicil to Casaubon's will. Ladislaw is recognised by Raffles, who tells him that his mother ran away from her family. Raffles next goes to Bulstrode's, and we learn through Bulstrode's own consciousness the truth about his own past – he had married the widow of his employer, had had serious qualms about the nature of the pawnbroker's business he carried on for them, and had concealed the fact that he knew the whereabouts of the widow's daughter and her son since he, Bulstrode, was certain that the widow would not marry him if the daughter were found. Bulstrode sends for Will and tells him the truth, seeking to atone, but Will rejects him, and afterwards Bulstrode weeps like a child. Meanwhile Dorothea thinks of Will, provoked to by Mrs Cadwallader and Sir James, and Will comes to take another last goodbye. Dorothea realises that he is renouncing her but loves her; Will leaves impetuously.

Commentary

Chapter 54
Dorothea's reactions towards Celia's baby and her self-absorption are natural in view of her continuing inward suffering. Celia shoots a 'needle-arrow' of sarcasm when she learns that Dorothea is returning to Lowick. There is some delightful authorial irony at the expense of Sir James suggesting that they all go to Cheltenham, since 'at that period a man could hardly know what to propose if Cheltenham were rejected'. Mrs Cadwallader points out stingingly to Dorothea exactly what kind of madness she will endure if she sits alone at Lowick, and also sets about her usual matchmaking role of finding someone to marry Dorothea. In an expressive image the notebooks in the library at Lowick are compared to 'the weary waste plated with huge stones, the mute memorial of a forgotten faith'. A remarkable insight into Dorothea's sense of duty follows, her thoughts almost becoming a dialogue with her dead husband, while she writes him a note to say that she cannot work at what she does not believe in. The actions are consistent with Dorothea's close questioning of herself throughout.

She feels guilty about her 'motiveless ease', and an unforced dramatic irony plays over her first meeting with Will, where even the servant Pratt knows the content of the codicil. Dorothea presumes Will knows too, but his impulsive reactions are set against her own recognition that she will miss him if he goes away. His anger makes him feel 'as if they were like two creatures slowly turning to marble in each other's presence' for he has imposed constraints upon himself, and of course the world sees constraints placed upon him by Casaubon's will. Dorothea's naïvety and Will's bloody-mindedness and over-reaction make the offer of the miniature a barrier rather than a bond between them. The entrance of Sir James is dramatically effective, stilling the emotion of each and unconsciously ensuring that 'Will's pride became a repellent force, keeping him asunder from Dorothea.'

Chapter 55
Dorothea finds herself seeking consolation in the miniature which she had offered Will and which consciously replaces him as she puts it before her. Even now she does not realise that she is in love, and the dialogue involving the Chettams and Mrs Cadwallader is spiced with a fine innuendo and wit on the subject of first and second marriages. Sir James, with his particular sensitivity on Dorothea's account, finds the subject distasteful, but Dorothea's taking off her widow's cap is a symbolic gesture, perhaps unconscious, of her leading a new life of practical idealism free from the directives of her husband.

Chapter 56
In Caleb she finds the right man to encourage practical works, but the historical linking with the wider world is here in the coming of the railway through Lowick. The resistance to change, as well as the motivation to make a good profit, are the twin pivots of Middlemarch opinion. Solomon Featherstone stirs up public reaction in the small hamlet of Frick against the coming of the railways, and again we note the connective with the wider political issues in this small political action which is resisting, if you like, change, progress, reform. This ultimately brings about the scene in which the haymakers turn on the agents. Fred shows his spirit by driving away the men, and then a willingness to help Caleb Garth with the measuring which undoubtedly puts thoughts into Caleb's mind about doing something for Fred. The latter has the delicious sense 'that he should be courting Mary when he was helping her father'.

Caleb deals promptly with the men, but the social divisions are clearly enunciated by one of the labourers, Timothy Cooper, who points out that canals and railways do not improve the lot of the poor man. When Fred has helped him Caleb himself spells out the work-ethic by which he lives – a man must always do well 'what he undertook to do'. Fred's confession of his love for Mary moves Caleb, and their dialogue shows the frank honesty in Fred – he knows that his education has been a mistake – and the generous response of Caleb. Interaction between husband and wife is natural even down to the detail of Mrs Garth being 'secretly a little hurt' that Caleb has actually determined to take on Fred without consulting her. She has her own moment of power when she tells Caleb that Mary could have had Mr Farebrother, but Caleb's humility about himself, his sure insight into Mary's feelings, his expression of love for this wife who took him 'though I was a plain man' moves that wife to tears. Later Fred is humiliated – after all his education – to find that his writing is not up to standard, but when he tells his parents of his position with Caleb (Mrs Garth knows they will misunderstand) he is surprised by their different reactions. Mr Vincy tells him to 'stick to it', Mrs Vincy, scenting a Garth conspiracy, cries every time she looks at Fred for the next few days.

Chapter 57
The sonnet prefaced to the chapter is in praise of Sir Walter Scott, and is autobiographical in the sense that Marian Evans once had to take back a

Scott novel before she had finished it. The exact appropriateness to this chapter, with its evocation of happy family life, is seen when we find Jim Garth reading *Ivanhoe*. Fred has to listen to praise of Christy – who is in a way a direct reflection on him, through his diligence and application – but Mrs Garth, who has a sense of rightness and knows that her husband is soft, is intent on giving Fred a lesson, for 'her vexation had fermented the more actively because of its total repression towards her husband'. When she reveals Mr Farebrother's love for Mary to Fred she realises that she has gone too far, but Fred is able to escape under the chaos of the children's activities. The insight into Mrs Garth's inward reactions is acute, into Fred's intuitively right, as he realises that he has a rival and that Mary is staying at the Parsonage. The interaction there makes him jealous, and he feels that the family are all conspiring in the affair when Mr Farebrother, generous in spirit as ever, contrives to leave Fred and Mary alone. Fred is aggressive, Mary piquant and teasing, but she draws Fred's attention directly to Mr Farebrother's delicacy of feeling. Left alone, Mary has some temptation towards the thought of Mr Farebrother, but knows that really she can only love Fred.

Chapter 58
Rosamond's obstinacy and her false sense of values lead to the loss of her baby, and Lydgate is to be undermined by this obstinacy, which he hadn't expected. Rosamond's snobbery is seen in the way she feels that when she introduced Captain Lydgate to her guests 'his rank penetrated them as if it has been an odour'. Rosamond enjoys the flirtation, and thinks that Ladislaw doesn't come because he is jealous of Captain Lydgate (a fop and bore). Lydgate himself has now come to some realisation of his position, that his wife does not 'reverence her husband's mind', is hurt by her riding, has the delicacy not to blame her when she loses her baby after riding again, but 'he secretly wondered over the terrible tenacity of this mild creature' whose 'affection did not make her compliant'. The water imagery carries its own moral comment, for Lydgate's marital subjection is 'as noxious to him as an inlet of mud to a creature that has been used to breathe and bathe and dart after its illuminated prey in the clearest of waters'. Not only is he able to dedicate less time to his studies, he also has the knowledge that Rosamond has no consciousness that they are in debt. Lydgate's own careless assumption is based on the fact that he 'walked by habit, not by self-criticism'. His inward drama is balanced by the outward drama of the need to tell Rosamond.

Again appropriate imagery characterises his mistake, the effects being at work within him 'like a recognised chronic disease'. Ironically, Will's sensitivity means that he has a clearer insight into Lydgate and his mood than Rosamond. In a remarkable backward glance Lydgate invokes Laure's action as he looks at the 'feminine impassibility' of Rosamond, thinking 'Would *she* kill me because I wearied her?' He also thinks of Dorothea's plea to him for advice. His approach to Rosamond indicates his kindness and the reawakening of his first love for her; she responds by laying her

hand on his, and by being 'conscious of forgiving him'. Her lack of understanding of her husband is shown when she says that she will ask her father
for the money. Her chill attitude, although she returns his kiss 'faintly',
already throws a gloom over the future which Lydgate knows he must
endure.

Chapter 59
Lydgate's delicacy is stressed, for he believes that Dorothea and Will are
passionately attached to each other, and hence will not gossip about them.
He knows about the codicil to Casaubon's will, and with admirable sensitivity tells Rosamond not to mention it to Will. Rosamond, obstinate and
flirtatious at the same time, deliberately ignores his advice and also deceives
him over her father, whom she asks for money. This short chapter marks
an important plot revelation; Will is now in an even more intolerable position with regard to Dorothea than he was before.

Chapter 60
This chapter also is important to the plot. Firstly, there is the fine festival
atmosphere attendant upon the Larcher sale. Will, made obstinate by his
new knowledge, takes some delight in appearing publicly, almost as a challenge to those who know about Casaubon's will. But running with Will's
silent attendance to purchase the painting for Mrs Bulstrode is the humorous rhetoric of Mr Trumbull. Mr Trumbull is quick to improvise upon
stray remarks from his audience and is not lacking in wit himself. Even the
joke about ladybirds, honey, and money he manages to explain as 'a
sting – it has what we call satire, and wit without indecency'. Raffles's
appearance, and his staring so markedly at Will, gives a dramatic edge to
the purchase of the painting; later Raffles provides the information that
Will's mother ran away because she was ashamed of her connection with
the 'high style of receiving house' run by her parents.

Chapter 61
The influence of the past on the present is nowhere more agonisingly
demonstrated in *Middlemarch* than in this chapter. The appearance of
Raffles at his home has made Bulstrode ill; inwardly stricken, he acknowledges his wife's goodness outwardly, a touching foretaste of that goodness
she shows when the real crisis comes upon them. There is a sure and subtle
insight into their relationship, she not eager to know of his past, he knowing and understanding this in his 'ingenuous' wife, whose imitative piety
and native worldliness were equally sincere'. Bulstrode's wish is that providence may send 'death to hinder him' (Raffles) from returning to Middlemarch, the irony being that providence is later going to put a direct
temptation in Bulstrode's way. The laying bare of Bulstrode's consciousness
is superbly done, with the 'web' of the past woven into the suffering of the
present.
     The use of retrospect deepens our knowledge of the man, who has
fought his own battle with his conscience in that past when he discovered

what kind of business he was in. He is able to reconcile his faith with this practice, goes through it all again in his mind, and here the image of the web is used to explain his self-justifying pleas, for 'the years had been perpetually spinning them into intricate thickness, like masses of spider-web, padding the moral sensibility'. But now Bulstrode is enmeshed in the dangerous revelations of a past which could undermine his present. His concealment that his previous wife's daughter had been found is another moral and spiritual sin in his own conscience, and his withdrawal from the degrading business means that his present prosperity is founded on money made from it. He reasons and prays himself into making what he thinks of as restitution, and writes to Will, who is immediately aware that this 'pale-eyed sickly-looking piece of respectability' is intent on looking back to that past which the unwelcome appearance of Raffles has stimulated both in himself and in Bulstrode.

Despite the latter's revelations, Will feels 'some pity which was half-contempt for this voluntary self-abasement of an elderly man'. Even here our compassion does not desert Bulstrode despite the revulsion we feel for his past actions. There is a further irony and a strong moral decision; Bulstrode's offer, if accepted by Will, would enable him to go to Dorothea as a man of independent means. Will, conscious of dishonour and remembering his mother's repudiation of her family's business, rejects the offer with his customary openness, brusquely unmindful of Bulstrode's present feelings but aware 'that it would have been impossible for him ever to tell Dorothea that he had accepted it'. There is a fine sense of dramatic immediacy about their exchanges, and a complete identification with the man we should hate – Bulstrode – whose weakness, self-righteousness and repentance alike are all essentially human.

Chapter 62
Will, in highly sensitive reaction to the news of his mother's family, feels that Dorothea's friends would look down upon him even more if they knew; meanwhile Sir James, who overdoes his brotherly interest in Dorothea, persuades Mrs Cadwallader to introduce the gossip that Will is constantly seeing Rosamond as a means of warning Dorothea. Dorothea's spirited reaction shows her feelings for Ladislaw, feelings which she had not fully acknowledged to herself. Her breaking down afterwards is a sure index to the depth of those feelings. The scene between Dorothea and Will is one of the finest in the novel; it underlines the fact that when two people are in love, their words may not lead them directly to each other in complete recognition of that love. Will feels passion, Dorothea a tremulous 'dangerous tendency to sob', but Will's 'hyperbole' is not fully grasped by Dorothea, who at one moment thinks he loves her but at the next is filled with uncertainty. She even feels he may be speaking of Rosamond. His final words convince her that he loves her; there is joy for her – and sadness – but Will is bitter, for he has 'no assurance that she loved him'.

BOOK VII   TWO TEMPTATIONS

Summary

Generously, and delicately, Farebrother, guessing that Lydgate has financial difficulties, offers to help him, but Lydgate's pride will not allow him to have the offer made openly. Rosamond's pride and obstinacy lead her to forestall Lydgate's attempts to pay some of his debts by economising; she writes to Sir Godwin Lydgate, who replies to Lydgate, thus humiliating him further. The division between Lydgate and Rosamond – who has twice acted behind his back – is now complete. Lydgate gambles, and is saved from losing too much by Fred's intervention, while Farebrother, revealing his own preference for Mary Garth, consigns her to Fred provided that he makes himself worthy of her. Lydgate sees Bulstrode, who announces that he is withdrawing from the Hospital, may move away, and that the Fever Hospital is likely to amalgamate with the Infirmary, though Dorothea may in fact take Bulstrode's place. Lydgate tries to get a loan from Bulstrode, who tells him that he ought to become a bankrupt.

The return of Raffles moves Bulstrode to immediate action to get rid of him; he asks Caleb to find a tenant for Stone Court, and Caleb puts forward Fred Vincy. Caleb finds Raffles ill at Stone Court, Bulstrode gets Lydgate to attend him, and Caleb gives up working for Bulstrode after what he has heard from Raffles. Lydgate says that Raffles must be given no liquor, Bulstrode watches over him, Lydgate returns later to prescribe opium, and Bulstrode decides to give him the loan of £1000. He lets the housekeeper give Raffles wine. When Lydgate arrives he cannot understand why Raffles is dead, and feels some unease. Gossip about Bulstrode spreads, Lydgate is implicated, Bulstrode is called upon to resign public positions, and Lydgate, out of compassion, helps him from the meeting. Dorothea resolutely asserts her faith in Lydgate.

Commentary

Chapter 63
Farebrother's friendliness and generosity of spirit with regard to Lydgate are stressed, and we note that the strains on Lydgate have led him into taking opium. The irony embraces the fact that no one could ever believe wrong of Rosamond or that she is anything but perfect. Once again a family gathering – here at the Vincys – allows of wider interaction, with Fred intent upon Mary as his mother watches her, and Mrs Vincy indiscreet in her reference to Lydgate having 'a close, proud disposition'. Again there is a striking emphasis on the dissonance between appearance and reality. Mary's natural warmth wins Mrs Vincy's youngest girls to her and brings about some softening in that lady's attitude. Lydgate reveals his irritability when Farebrother comes to thank him for recommending him for the Lowick living.

Chapter 64

The 'sordid cares' are telling on Lydgate, who feels the world narrowing around him through 'the miserable isolation of egoistic fears'. He sinks his pride in order to try to carry Rosamond along sympathetically with him, but 'in her secret soul she was utterly aloof from him'. Lydgate intends to rule but can't; in an ironic aside the author observes, 'The shallowness of a waternixie's soul may have a charm until she becomes didactic' and Rosamond, humiliated by the suggestion that Ned Plymdale may take their house, becomes didactic and circumvents her husband. This deception shows the inflexible nature of her egoism, her determination 'to hinder what Lydgate liked to do'. It is the beginning of the end of their love, despite Lydgate's suppressed anger and moments of rekindled tenderness. Rosamond has to take some satire from Mrs Plymdale, but rides it with her usual propriety although she is almost near a self-admission when she says that 'appearances have very little to do with happiness'.

There is further humour in the Trumbull manner when Rosamond goes to him. Rosamond herself lies, and can't resist telling Lydgate that the Plymdales have taken a house; it is a small triumph emblematic of the larger and coercive power she is going to wield domestically. Her second action is less successful, based as it is on snobbery and wrong-headedness. She writes to Sir Godwin, allowing him to think that she has her husband's sanction, and then has to tell Lydgate that she has countermanded his orders to Trumbull. The ensuing row is maintained at boiling temperature for Lydgate, effectively contrasted with Rosamond's voice 'that fell and trickled like cold water-drops'. Moreover, her 'torpedo contact' has undermined Lydgate. Her consciousness is examined in order to show just how far she is from Lydgate in sympathy, how little she understands his work, how she misses the flirtatious Will. By an ironic parallel, Lydgate is thinking of sinking his pride and paying a visit to Sir Godwin.

Chapter 65

Lydgate thinks of taking the railway to Quallingham, which is George Eliot's unobtrusive way of indicating the wider changes which are occurring, and which balance these small but important changes in private lives. Sir Godwin's letter humiliates Lydgate, disappoints Rosamond, but only hardens her inflexibility. Lydgate, whose conscience is ever active, still feels some guilt that by marrying her he has deserved her reproaches for the troubles that have come upon them. His love and his sense of responsibility are both strong. As he says, 'When I hurt you, I hurt part of my own life', and when she responds, 'I wish I had died with the baby' we know that she 'had mastered him' and that caresses cannot atone for their lack of loving contact.

Chapter 66

Lydgate still uses his sympathy – which is natural to him – on the needs of his patients, though he has no time because of his financial and marital worries to press on with his research. His reflexes draw him to opium and then to gambling though not with addiction to each; they are merely 'spots of commonness' as the pressures increase. Fred's 'small escape' to the billiard-room at the 'Green Dragon' leads him to the edge of betting temptation too, and there is an interesting contrast drawn between himself and Lydgate. Fred's moral education, however, has begun in earnest, and he is shocked by seeing the brother-in-law, whom he considers a prig, gambling.

He extricates Lydgate from his game, using Farebrother as the pretext, and Farebrother in turn brings moral pressure to bear on Fred, always thinking of Mary and that Fred must be worthy of her. In fact it is somewhat ironic, since Fred has not succumbed to the temptations of the 'Green Dragon'. Farebrother, with the best possible intentions, succeeds in shaking Fred. Rather than let him go to the dogs, Farebrother builds up his own chances with Mary as a means of getting Fred to behave with uprightness and responsibility. It is a fine and shrewd – and brave – piece of altruism, and Fred's response shows his own moral calibre when he says, 'I will try to be worthy . . . of you as well as of her.'

Chapter 67

Lydgate turns to Bulstrode with some self-disgust. It is the more difficult since he finds Bulstrode's religiosity contemptible, and it is an important motif in the plot, for later Bulstrode and Lydgate are to be associated in the public mind as guilty men. The running irony is that Bulstrode's interest in the hospital has waned in proportion to the fear of Raffles, something of which Lydgate is at this stage in ignorance.

Lydgate feels some justification in asking Bulstrode for money because the latter has 'indirectly helped to cause the failure of his practice', though he is tempted to entertain Rosamond's suggestion that he should sell that practice. Bulstrode, now positively hypochondriacal and fearing insanity, is reassured by Lydgate's diagnosis of his anxiety, and Lydgate is able to enter upon his own worries. But Bulstrode's absorbing egoism – and of course his decision to back away from his hospital responsibilities – do not make the moment propitious. Bulstrode considers the Vincys irresponsible, and his manner of rejecting Lydgate's appeal shows that despite his own worries he still enjoys playing God.

Chapter 68

Retrospect on Raffles's visit to Bulstrode's home on Christmas Eve integrates the reasons for his attitudes and decisions in the previous chapter. Motivated by fear of revelation, spending much 'of his wretchedness in prayer', Bulstrode gets rid of Raffles on Christmas Day. His mind is not at peace though, since he feels that his wife half suspects that he has a discreditable secret, and he makes provisional plans only, since if Raffles does disappear he will be able to resume his work in the name of God in Middlemarch. All this terrible introspection is contrasted with the generous outward response of Caleb Garth in his wishing to place Fred as the tenant of Stone Court. Meanwhile, with unconscious irony, Mrs Bulstrode gives her pity to poor Rosamond.

Chapter 69
Bulstrode moves into immediate crisis as Caleb Garth reveals that Raffles is at Stone Court and that he (Caleb) is giving up his management for Bulstrode. Even here Caleb is gentle, and feels 'a deep pity for him' though his remark that 'I would injure no man if I could help it ... even if I thought God winked at it' is unconsciously definitive of Bulstrode's own inward debate and failure in the past. Caleb also shows a keen insight into Bulstrode's struggle and wish to repent. There is an admirable simplicity and directness in what he says. It is clear that his own high moral code means that he has not condemned Bulstrode – 'I am ready to believe better, when better is proved.' He is suitably reserved with Mrs Garth when he tells her that he has given up his work for Bulstrode. The latter, relieved that it was Caleb and no other who has heard Raffles's story, continues to fight his inward battle, hoping 'that the will of God might be the death of that hated man'.

The deterioration in Raffles gives him some heart, though he can't get control over his mind. Lydgate's diagnosis of alcoholic poisoning unwittingly provides Bulstrode with the means of finishing Raffles, though there is the now-familiar battle with his conscience. Meanwhile, and before that event, Lydgate continues to suffer, much more on Rosamond's account than on his own. When he finds Dover's man in the house he goes straight to his prostrate wife with the moving appeal, 'Let us only love one another.' It is in vain; he is 'bruised and shattered', and Rosamond is chill.

Chapter 70
The rhyming couplet motto has direct reference to both Bulstrode and Lydgate, and therefore is a unifying strand in the structure. Bulstrode, intent on finding out all he can, searches Raffles's pockets. Raffles himself displays fear of Bulstrode, almost as if his delirium has a forecasting power of what is to come. Bulstrode intends to obey Lydgate's orders despite the obvious temptation not to – Raffles is always asking for brandy and will take no food. He thinks too of how to propitiate Lydgate, but there is a sympathetic immediacy about his consciousness which is moving and terribly conveyed by a sustained image:

> Strange, piteous conflict in the soul of this unhappy man, who had longed for years to be better than he was – who had taken his selfish passions into discipline and clad them in severe robes, so that he had walked with them as a devout quire, till now that a terror had risen among them, and they could chant no longer, but threw out their common cries for safety.

Without acknowledging temptation, even perhaps unaware of his own hypocrisy, Bulstrode gives Lydgate the cheque; afterwards both are uneasy, Lydgate because he is indebted, Bulstrode because he becomes aware of his own motivation.

The might-have-been element in the narrative is seen again as Bulstrode ponders whether he should go home. He doesn't, the fear that Mrs Abel may have given too much opium to Raffles already seizes him, he does nothing about it, and then undergoes 'A struggle'. And just as he has lost all his important struggles, so Bulstrode loses this one. He gives Mrs Abel the key to the wine-cooler, prays, caught in the web of his own wishes, for he had 'not yet unravelled in his thought the confused promptings of the last four-and-twenty hours'. Though Lydgate is uneasy, thinking that he has misjudged the case, he and Bulstrode talk of the wider issues in the world outside, like the Reform Bill in the House of Lords, a telling contrast with the unreformed nature of man, whose weaknesses involve corruption and death. Farebrother generously acknowledges Bulstrode's goodness in advancing the money to Lydgate, though he had advised Lydgate to avoid 'any personal entanglement' with him.

Chapter 71
What starts as a lounging debate about horseflesh outside the 'Green Dragon' escalates into the revelations about Bulstrode, much to the delight of his main enemy of note, Mr Frank Hawley. It spreads through the community 'like the smell of fire', news that Caleb has given up working for Bulstrode adds more fuel, and the speed of the narrative matches the speed of the news. Farebrother faced with Hawley conceals Lydgate's attendance at Stone Court out of friendship and a generous decency to believe the best. Mrs Bulstrode herself reveals the loan innocently, 'moral grounds' of suspicion that there is collusion between Lydgate and Bulstrode are ignited, and Mrs Dollop contributes her own mite of certainty that Bulstrode 'was forced to take Old Harry into his counsel, and Old Harry's been too many for him'.

The lower orders of Middlemarch embark on the natural current of distortion which succeeds in making something of a hero of the disreputable Raffles. This is comic commentary, but the 'principal townsmen' have serious moral intentions, and the meeting of the sanitary board (another reference to contemporary Parliamentary legislation) gives convenient occasion for the public indictment of Bulstrode. Lydgate is sensitive to the atmosphere when he and Bulstrode enter the meeting together. With Hawley's attack, Lydgate is moved to compassion – he is always the doctor – by the 'shrunken misery of Bulstrode's livid face'. Nevertheless Bulstrode has 'the strength of reaction'. The 'flame' 'was beginning to stir and glow under his ashy paleness', but his counter-accusation of 'chicanery' in others is immediately rebutted by Hawley. Lydgate's action of help was 'unspeakably bitter to him', for he realises that it puts him, in the eyes of everyone present, with Bulstrode – just as he had been over the question of the hospital chaplaincy. It is left to Dorothea to express her energetic faith in him, and we are left with the impression that at last she has something positive, calling out her deepest needs to serve the cause of truth.

BOOK VIII   SUNSET AND SUNRISE

Summary

Farebrother is cautious, Dorothea intent on action, mainly because of what Lydgate has done for her. Lydgate meanwhile broods deeply in his isolation, knowing that his action will be misconstrued, wondering how Rosamond will 'take it all'. Mrs Bulstrode learns of her husband's disgrace, and movingly decides to stand by him without reproach (see Chapter 5 of this commentary). Will writes to Lydgate to say he will be visiting Middlemarch, Rosamond sends out invitations which are declined, and her father tells her the news. Lydgate is jarred by Rosamond's lack of sympathy; all she wants to do is to leave Middlemarch. Dorothea hears Lydgate's story and expresses her belief in him. She offers to go to see Rosamond, does so, delivers a letter for Lydgate and finds Ladislaw alone with Rosamond. Will, aware of the unfortunate interpretation Dorothea may put upon this, lacerates Rosamond verbally after Dorothea has left.

Dorothea, alone, gives way to her now recognised love for Will. She spends a terrible night, but determines to put aside her own anguish and go to see Rosamond again. Lydgate meets her, thanks her for the cheque (which enables him to pay Bulstrode) and Dorothea, alone with Rosamond, tells her of her faith in her husband and how concerned he is on her (Rosamond's) account. Rosamond, greatly moved, tells Dorothea that Will loves her (Dorothea). Rosamond writes to Will, and Will and Dorothea acknowledge their love for each other. Sir James disapproves. Bulstrode arranges for Fred to manage Stone Court, Mary tells Fred this news, the last chapter ending with their happiness.

Commentary

Chapter 72
Farebrother calls upon his experience of dealing with Lydgate on personal matters in order to move Dorothea's defence of him to a more cautious approach. Dorothea, intent on making 'life less difficult to each other', is still ardent, but is faced with Sir James's protective partisanship and Farebrother's wise definition – that character 'is something living and changing, and may become diseased as our bodies do'. The appropriateness of the metaphor, while not directly applicable to Lydgate, reflects Farebrother's sensitivity and his own concern for Dorothea. Faced with Celia's common sense as well, Dorothea bursts into 'angry tears', an index to her still nervous state and the fact that she is being denied an outlet for her warm and sympathetic nature.

Chapter 73
Lydgate himself feels a rage at his lot. He feels that his marriage is 'an unmitigated calamity', but the author's corollary to this is even more pertinent to his state:

Only those who know the supremacy of the intellectual life – the life which has a seed of ennobling thought and purpose within it – can understand the grief of one who falls from that serene activity into the absorbing soul-wasting struggle with worldly annoyances.

He weighs the pros and cons of Bulstrode's behaviour, finding in his own position a 'benumbing cruelty', and he also examines his own motives in *not* inquiring more closely into the death of Raffles. He is made even more miserable by the fact that he doubts whether his fellow practitioners would question themselves as closely as he is doing. He also feels that the taint of guilt will always cling to him in Middlemarch. He determines to brave it out, appalled however that he cannot tell Rosamond and that he is bound by her 'dumb mastery'.

Chapter 74

The finely ironic opening to one of the finest chapters in the book, with public opinion strongly reflected in individuals whose 'various moral impulses were called into play which tended to stimulate utterance'. The irony embraces that word of many motives, 'candour', as well as 'the love of truth', and the 'moral improvements' or 'soul' of the friend who needs to be helped. Gossip in the superior houses is generally sympathetic towards 'poor Harriet', though there is much speculation as to what she will do when she discovers the truth. Mrs Bulstrode in crisis transcends all gossip, but before that she has some intuition that her husband's troubles are emotional and mental rather than physical, and she is not convinced by Lydgate's white lie on the subject. Her visit to Mrs Hackbutt, where she bravely tries to find out what is wrong, produces nothing of substance, while her call on Mrs Plymdale convinces her that there is something of a very serious nature, and she leaves, not wishing to let her old friend be explicit about it.

Mr Vincy senses at a glance that she knows everything, and then is forced to tell her since she knows nothing, a dramatic and poignant stroke in the narrative. Before this she has a vision of her husband disgraced, and sees herself 'at his side in mournful but unreproaching fellowship with shame and isolation'. It is an exact forecast of what happens, a wonderful movement into her consciousness and its self-knowledge. Vincy himself shows her a 'rough but well-meaning affectionateness'. A commentary on her reactions is given in Chapter 5 of this book. It is a remarkable instance of George Eliot's identification with character at one of the supreme crises of life – truthful, sympathetic, movingly and unerringly done.

Chapter 75

Rosamond's consciousness is exposed, her 'secret repulsion' for her husband because of what he has failed to give her providing an unpleasant moral contrast to her aunt's actions in the previous chapter. She had built up a little romance for herself, her natural egoism and vanity telling her that Will Ladislaw, despite quitting Middlemarch, would secretly come to prefer her to Dorothea. This is another link in the ultimate unravelling of the plot. When Ladislaw writes, Rosamond's face 'looked like a reviving flower – it grew prettier and more blooming'. Her evening party invitations are another deception, albeit in minor key. The contrast with her aunt is deepened when she has to learn the truth about her husband and Bulstrode. Vincy again shows himself a generous and feeling man.

At home Rosamond is even more distant, and the water imagery, once evocative of life, is here used with a subtle twist to indicate a living death – 'it was as if they were both adrift on one piece of wreck and looked away from each other'. She expects Lydgate to speak, he expects her faith in him, and again we are reminded of Harriet Bulstrode and her voiced forgiveness of her husband who has not spoken. With strong self-discipline Lydgate finds self-control enough to speak to his wife – she, before he can say anything, urges that they move to London. 'They lived on from day to day with their thoughts still apart'; emotionally they are even further apart, Lydgate angry and surly, Rosamond chill and withdrawn.

Chapter 76

Dorothea – 'her emotions were imprisoned' – has asked Lydgate to call on her, intent upon finding out the truth from him and defending him if possible. She immediately notices the change in his appearance, and speaks directly, openly, and to him movingly, of her belief in him. Lydgate responds to the nobility and warmth of her nature, tells her all, and Dorothea in turn responds by saying that she will clear his name – 'There is nothing better that I can do in the world.' Lydgate dwells on the details of the Raffles' case and the adhering suspicion, considers himself 'blighted – like a damaged ear of corn' – while Dorothea fully understands not only his feelings here, but his idealism, 'to love what is great, and try to reach it, and yet to fail'. Dorothea suggests the compromise that Lydgate should stay and get the hospital going with the backing of her money – we note her consistent obsession to *give* – but Lydgate is moved to confess obliquely his other trouble, a trouble which he senses Dorothea will comprehend because of her own suffering in the same sphere – that of marriage.

Dorothea's 'keen memory of her own life' and her intuition of the 'invisible barriers' between Lydgate and Rosamond which he can only refer to obliquely moves her to the generous offer of going to see Rosamond and clearing her husband's name to her. Lydgate accepts this, but insists that he must leave Middlemarch; he forecasts his future accurately, but with a terrible sense of bitterness – we feel the knife-edge of his failure, the pressures which he knows will come from Rosamond for conformity and income as against idealism – for he knows he must 'set up in a watering-place, or go to some southern town where there are plenty of idle English, and get myself puffed, that is the sort of shell I must creep into and try to keep my soul alive in'. When he leaves he realises the uniqueness of Dorothea – that she has 'what I never saw in any woman before – a fountain of friendship towards men – a man can make a friend of her'. She also has the immediate generosity – and sensitivity – to promise him the cheque.

Chapter 77
A poignant and dramatic shift to Rosamond, now melancholy and hoping
that Ladislaw will come to see her and relieve the monotony of her existence. Her 'ennui' and the sadness attendant upon it has even made her
husband 'timid' of speaking to her. Meanwhile Dorothea thinks of her
visit, of Will's previous visits to Rosamond, and takes some assurance that
the final words he spoke indicated a passionate devotion to her, Dorothea.
She also feels strongly resistant to what is said about Will – part of the
Bulstrode–Lydgate revelations – 'in that part of her world which lay within
park palings'. Her thoughts and feelings for Will are deep and she has not
renounced him despite their separation. She goes to Rosamond intent on
relieving her loneliness and making a friend of her. The visit is fraught with
drama for her for she sees 'in the terrible illumination of a certainty which
filled up all outlines' Will Ladislaw clasping a tearful Rosamond's hands in
his own. Will sees 'Dorothea's eyes with a new lightning in them', but with
commendable firmness Dorothea leaves the letter for Lydgate and goes,
knowing as she drives away that 'She had never felt anything like this
triumphant power of indignation in the struggle of her married life.' It is
remarkable, showing us her resilience, the transference of anger and hurt
into positive action and endeavour. This is Dorothea – capable of being
injured but always, with courage and energy, rising above it in the cause of
serving others.

Chapter 78
Rosamond is rather gratified by what has happened, but Will's reaction is
predictably extreme – he won't let Rosamond touch him, wants to lacerate
her with words, but holds back. He does vent his anger on Rosamond, but
the effect is not helped by the imagery as he moves 'with the restlessness
of a wild animal that sees prey but cannot reach it'. Once started he cannot stop before he says: 'I would rather touch her hand if it were dead,
than I would touch any other woman's living.' This is gall to Rosamond,
whose little fantasy has been poisoned; Lydgate's return, his genuine concern for her in her illness of reaction, and the irony in that he feels she
may have been more concerned for him after Dorothea's visit: all this is
packed into the dramatic ending of the chapter.

Chapter 79
Lydgate's disclosure to Will that his name is part of the current rumours in
Middlemarch brings forther a sardonic rejoinder from Ladislaw. Again the
irony is present, Will having the reticence not to reveal that he, unlike
Lydgate, had rejected Bulstrode's offer of money. He is also moved, but
pities Lydgate (and himself) when he learns of Dorothea's faith in Lydgate.

Chapter 80
Dorothea's reaction is to throw herself into practical activity, visiting the
school and Mr Farebrother, talking of his interests in nature, a delightful
authorial aside considering creatures 'that converse compendiously with
their antennae, and for aught we know may hold reformed parliaments',
thus linking once more the small histories with the large at the time.

Henrietta Noble's devotion to Ladislaw is made an innocent reflection of Dorothea's own but, when she is alone, Dorothea gives way to her feelings in moaning out: 'Oh, I did love him.' Imagery of waves, plants, and seeds conveys the anguished movements of her feeling, and she lies on the bare floor, 'while her grand woman's frame was shaken by sobs as if she had been a despairing child'. There is a terrifying image of a bleeding child cut in two. The 'fire' of her anger 'flames out', but when she wakes in the night she is determined not to sit 'in the narrow cell of her calamity'.

The packed sequence of images exactly conveys the crowded nature of Dorothea's experienced suffering. She puts it aside, and thinks of 'those three' – Lydgate, Rosamond and Will. She feels the 'light', looks out through the 'window' – both symbols of an awakening to altruism and the putting aside of self – and sees 'the largeness of the world and the manifold wakings of men to labour and endurance'. Just as Mrs Bulstrode resumed her old plain dress as a token of her new hard life, so Dorothea chooses a new one as token of the newer and greater life of giving she is about to undertake.

Chapter 81

Dorothea's second visit to Rosamond provides one of the finest scenes in *Middlemarch*, though 'scene' does not quite convey the emotional, moral and humanitarian nature of an exchange in which the generosity of the spirit in altruistic concern (Dorothea's) calls forth from petty egoism (Rosamond) a like if transitory response. Rosamond is in a state of 'new humiliating uncertainty', but she judges Dorothea's visit, as we might expect, wrongly, and her appearance when she sees Dorothea contributes to the irony of the situation – she is 'the lovely ghost of herself' with her 'rounded infantine mouth', all 'suggesting mildness and innocence'. Dorothea typically is hardly able to control her tears, but 'the emotion only passed over her face like the spirit of a sob'.

Rosamond immediately sees that all is not as she expected; her moral education, albeit temporary, has begun. One fine touch expresses Dorothea's 'motherliness', but the 'warm stream' of her generous, considered, wonderfully sensitive and sympathetic vindication of Lydgate to the wife who has not vindicated him in her own petty egoism, draws a response from Rosamond, at first limited by the propriety by which her life is conducted; when she bursts into hysterical crying we are aware that she is not merely crying from *self*, but because the emotional generosity of Dorothea has moved her to feel something that lies too deep for tears. The simple statement, 'Pride was broken down between these two' conveys the fact without the complexity of motives on both sides which has produced it.

Dorothea detects 'a faint pleasure' in Rosamond which is derived from the fact that she tells her that Lydgate feels he can no longer stay in Middlemarch. Her analysis of marriage – 'There is something even awful in the nearness it brings' leading to the 'I know it may be very dear – but it murders our marriage – and then the marriage stays with us like a murder

- and everything else is gone', reflects her uncompromising honesty. The truth for Dorothea is going to become a terrible truth for Rosamond – who is to be her husband's basil plant and feed on his brains. Again we are aware of the structural unity, but the emotional temperature does not drop – Dorothea's grasp of Rosamond's hands, Rosamond's kissing Dorothea's forehead – these are each an index to the pressure of a greater emotion than either has known.

Imagery of waves and shipwreck convey the perilous agitation of both women before Rosamond makes the one generous action of her life in order to reassure Dorothea that Will loves her. Lydgate's reappearance comes as an anticlimax to all that has passed between Dorothea and Rosamond; the latter shows Lydgate a reflex of warmth – part of Dorothea's influence is still there – but the chapter ends with Lydgate's 'sad resignation', almost a confirmation of Dorothea's definition of the marriage state given so unequivocally under the pressure of her emotion.

Chapter 82

Will reveals that he has a motive other than seeing Dorothea in returning to Middlemarch, namely to reconsider Bulstrode's offer of money and employ it on a project he has for work in the Far East. This seems unlikely enough, but at least it humanises Will and makes his moral rectitude seem fallible. After the scene with Rosamond he is a prey to conflicting desires of whether to stay or go – he knows that despite the revulsion he feels for Rosamond's attachment to him, he must also try to heal the friendship, as much on Lydgate's account as on hers. He sees himself as suffering 'discontented subjection', but Dorothea's action in going to Rosamond has ensured that the 'stealthy convergence of human lots' is to be effected for herself and Will, though each is in ignorance of this.

Chapter 83

The fine motto from John Donne's *The Good-Morrow* sounds the dominant note of this chapter. Dorothea's restlessness is described (with not a little irony that she has no immediate good works to concentrate on). Henrietta Noble is the means of bringing Will to her, but before that, and as she waits, feeling that to receive him in the library would be to act still under her husband's prohibition, she thinks, 'If I love him too much it is because he has been used so ill.' He is timid, Dorothea uncertain, but their first moving exchange is followed by their contemplation of the coming outside storm as the trees are tossed and the first lightning comes. It is a fine symbolic stroke – the storm is reflective of their own anguish on each other's account, but it is also the breaking which, so to speak, will clear the air for their love. The realism of the dialogue is occasionally undermined by Will's capacity for hyperbole, but the accompanying storm – 'the light seemed to be the terror of a hopeless love' – ensures that they must remain together, here in these moments and, prophetically, for ever. Will's impetuosity provokes the avowal from Dorothea: 'I don't mind about poverty – I hate my wealth.' There is indeed a 'good-morrow,' for they will have each other.

Chapter 84

A historical notation – 'It was just after the Lords had thrown out the Reform Bill' – reminds us as ever in *Middlemarch* of the wider world. The gossip about this, paralleled by Celia's about her baby, gives way dramatic- ally to Mr Brooke's entrance with the immediate 'sad news', which he puts off telling with his usual vacillation, being easily led into convenient side- tracks. Sir James gets himself into a state of 'white indignation' when he learns of Dorothea's impending marriage, but his hyperbole springs from his own interest in Dorothea and an inability to shift his grounds of status and behaviour. His anger and refusal to see Dorothea diminish this one- time 'amiable baronet' for the reader. Even Lady Chettam is moved to give 'royal evidence' that Dorothea had said that she would not marry again. Mrs Cadwallader takes a common-sense view, while her husband, as we might expect from his previous sensitivity, takes an enlightened one, observing: 'I must take Ladislaw's part until I hear more harm of him.' Celia, intent on seeing Dorothea, cannot move her from her determination, and there is a running authorial irony about Sir James's refusal to meet Ladislaw, and in Celia's horrified idea that Dorothea may be forced to 'always live in a street'.

Chapter 85

This marks a return to Bulstrode's consciousness and the effects that the revelations about him have had on his life and his wife's. Anxious to make amends, he feels the more keenly – as does his wife – the return of Lydgate's cheque. But the rounding off of this plot strand is accomplished by Bulstrode making amends through Harriet and seeing that Fred, supervised by Caleb, is to be put into Stone Court.

Chapter 86

The loving scene between Mary and her father as he tells her that Fred is to manage Stone Court for his aunt Bulstrode is given in convincing and moving dialogue. When he speaks of Mary's marriage Caleb's voice 'shook just perceptibly', and the whole atmosphere is conveyed with natural ease, the children, as ever, interacting with the adults, who are at last to find happiness. George Eliot's own view of the Garths' importance as the moral pivot of the novel, and the importance of the reclamation of Fred – who now becomes part of the work-ethic – is seen in her recurrence to them for the final chapter of *Middlemarch*.

FINALE

Summary

This is simply a rounding off by glances into the future lives of the charac- ters whose experiences we have shared, but with authorial apology for the limitations of perspective through the image central to *Middlemarch* – 'For the fragment of a life, however typical, is not the sample of an even web.' The focus is on marriages, with the Fred–Mary union both practically and idealistically treated, Fred subserving the work-ethic of the Garths, never becoming rich, but certainly happy. Lydgate died when he was fifty, having written a treatise on gout; thought to be successful, but conscious of his failure, his bitter equation of Rosamond as his 'basil plant' sufficiently indicates the authorial irony at her continuing undermining of her husband. Such is the way of the world that Rosamond makes a successful second marriage.

Will gets into Parliament (the constituency pays his expenses), Dorothea has a son who ultimately inherits Mr Brooke's estates and though Dorothea may be a 'foundress of nothing', we are told that 'the effect of her being on those around her was incalculably diffusive' of good.

Commentary

This rounding off sounds a note of qualified optimism, despite the failure of Lydgate and the partial failure of Dorothea; two happy marriages (three if we count the Chettams) underline the need for giving and working, with the inflexibility of a certain kind of egoism – Rosamond's – always capable of stifling relationships as well as idealism. The final paragraph stresses the sublime quality of individual goodness, the altruism which is a higher moral ideal in practice than the achievement of ambition.

3 THEMES AND ISSUES

3.1 THE POLITICAL BACKGROUND

The fictional content of *Middlemarch* is set against the historical reality of given time; the events which influence the characters of the novel occur within a chronology which runs from September 1829 until May 1832. In a fine article, first published in the first issue of *Victorian Studies* ('History by Indirection: the era of reform in *Middlemarch*'), Jerome Beaty has demonstrated the 'pervasiveness' of George Eliot's historical details and how she has managed 'to keep them, numerous as they are, from obtruding upon the fiction'.

The first Reform Bill was finally passed in June 1832, after the action of the novel (with the exception of the Finale) is complete. The novel thus traces through occasional reference the prelude to it. The Tory Minister Sir Robert Peel, who fought against it, is mentioned on the issue of Catholic Emancipation. He had changed his mind in favour of the Bill in March 1829, a few months before the novel begins, but there are several references to him in relation to Casaubon, who had 'written a very good pamphlet for Peel' on the subject of Catholic Emancipation. As Beaty points out, dating is in fact specific from time to time; in chapter 32 Peel comes into his father's title. This is in factual time on 3 May 1830 while Peter Featherstone is dying in fictional time, his funeral being at the end of the month (chapter 34). The Duke of Wellington is associated with Peel over Catholic Emancipation, and he too is mentioned – on four occasions. The casual, or seemingly casual, references occur throughout, and are an unobtrusive way of linking great events with small lives and thus establishing a convincing historical context for *Middlemarch*.

The death of George IV is prepared for in the text, but not mentioned directly apart from reference to 'the last bulletin concerning the King' (chapter 35) at about the time of Peter Featherstone's death. In fact the King died on 26 June 1830, while three chapters later Mr Brooke quotes Lafitte's remark 'Since yesterday, a century has passed away' (factually 29 July 1830) a reference to the July revolution in France and the overthrow of the French monarchy. By chapter 46 of the novel people were declaring that a Reform Bill would never be carried by the actual Parliament. This therefore looks forward to the dissolution of that Parliament on 22 April 1831, paving the way for elections which would ultimately lead to the passing of the Bill *and*, important to the plot of the novel, Mr Brooke's offering himself as a prospective candidate and making his ill-advised speech (as far as he gets through it) from the balcony of the White Hart.

Thereafter there is sparse mention of historical events, but chapter 84 begins with 'It was just after the Lords had thrown out the Reform Bill', an action which is completely overshadowed by Mr Brooke's announcement of Dorothea's impending marriage to Will. The Reform Bill itself, as Beaty rightly stresses, 'occurs off the Middlemarch stage', though the fictional time of Dorothea's wedding is very close to it, thus neatly rounding off the epoch of fictional lives and historical reality at one and the same time. Again it shows that meticulous attention to structure, that sense of unity, which characterises *Middlemarch*.

3.2 THE MEDICAL BACKGROUND

If the historical background is unobtrusively documented, then the medical background – perhaps more correctly foreground – is equally impressive, and again the strand of unity is evident in its deliberate stress. Lydgate himself seems to derive from Dr Clifford Allbutt, who was visited at his hospital in Leeds by George Eliot and Lewes in September 1868. He had been physician there since 1861, and the Leeds Home of Recovery was one of the first fever hospitals in the country, thus approximating to the Fever Hospital in Middlemarch originally sponsored by Bulstrode and his committee where Lydgate works without payment, the town's physicians turning their backs on it and refusing to work with Lydgate anyway. As Anna Kitchel observes, ' "Reform" was the watchword of the time, and the reform movement was invading medical circles as well as the political world.'

A study of George Eliot's *Quarry for Middlemarch* (the part designated *Quarry I* by Professor Kitchel) provides quotations from *The Lancet* which list the names of scientists and medical researchers from the past who influenced Lydgate, like Vesalius (1513–64) and Bichat (1771–1802). There is a detailed account of the treatment advocated in the case of typhus (which Fred Vincy contracts, Lydgate treats, and gets himself engaged as a result); there is Casaubon's heart disease, Raffles's delirium tremens (Lydgate's instructions to Bulstrode are ahead of his time, with the added irony that Bulstrode's disobedience of them would have been approved by Lydgate's medical contemporaries), Mr Trumbull's pneumonia and Nanny's cramps as a result of her starvation diet. George Eliot has Lydgate's medical training at Edinburgh and Paris; the first is praised in *The Lancet*, while at Paris bodies were available for dissection. Lydgate waxes lyrically to Rosamond on this aspect of his studies, and Rosamond responds with her customary finicky distaste.

Lydgate is the new kind of doctor, his studies in Paris leading him to favour new treatments for fever (listed in the *Quarry*), and he is also reformist in his use of the stethoscope and in his decision to prescribe without dispensing drugs. He is also zealous (and perhaps misguided) enough to wish to undertake post-mortems instead of the coroner, who, after all, was not a medical man. Something else listed which is certainly relevant to *Middlemarch* is the incidence of cholera in 1831–2. George Eliot gives the figures for cholera cases in London as 1530 by the end of March 1832, with 902 deaths, and it is interesting to note that in 1866, some three or four years before she began writing *Middlemarch*, there was another severe outbreak of cholera in this country. The medical background, the *avant garde* nature of Lydgate's theories and ideals, is as important to the overall conception of the novel as the political and historical range of reference which, like it, give the fictional lives authenticity.

3.3 SOCIETY BACKGROUNDS

In his excellent introduction to *Middlemarch*, W. J. Harvey lists the social categories embraced by the novel. *Middlemarch* is based on Coventry, but he points out that the historical time of the novel is not merely that of 1829–32, but also partakes of the period up to and including the time of writing, namely 1869–72, and that it thus takes account of the Second Reform Bill of 1867, which further extended the franchise. Ladislaw, he considers, is more of a later time than 1830, having a certain pre-Raphaelitish quality about him. None the less the main concern of the novel is with 'the relatively cramped and narrow society of England just before the Reform Bill of 1832', with the political climate serving to bring together, albeit temporarily, those of different classes, namely doctor, banker, businessman, manufacturer, cleric, man of leisure and baronet, to indicate the main areas. And there is also the major question of the outsider – Ladislaw, half-Polish and eccentric, Lydgate, man of family but intent on making himself great in his profession, and Bulstrode, twenty-five years a Middlemarcher but concealing a guilty past.

Birth, rank, class are central; Rosamond sees the Miss Brookes getting out of a carriage, but is not of a social equality with them. Chettam, the Cadwalladers and Mr Brooke, for example, can recognise Mr Vincy as Mayor, but would not recognise his family. So rooted is Chettam, far from an 'amiable baronet' in the class sense, that he cannot approve of Dorothea's marriage to Ladislaw, does his best to hinder it and is only reconciled by the pressures of Celia after Dorothea has had a baby. The Vincys look down on the Garths – Fred is a university man, Rosamond the flower of Mrs Lemon's – whereas Mary is a governess-cum-teacher as is her mother, who also prepares the family food. Mr Vincy, who is hard-pushed financially, is something of a bridge between the families in spite of himself, for rather than having Fred idle and on his hands he doesn't object to him apprenticing himself to Caleb Garth.

In *Middlemarch*, money rules, whether it is inherited or whether it is acquired. Thus Mr Brooke can live in leisure and fail to reform his own estates while preaching reform in his morally impecunious way; but *Middlemarch* foreshadows changes ('this is a world on the move', says Harvey), for Brooke is confronted by a recalcitrant tenant Dagley, who understands reform as little as his landlord does. Bulstrode can buy his way on to committees, can purchase Stone Court, but cannot buy Caleb Garth, a way into heaven, or even buy off Raffles. Peter Featherstone can buy sycophancy and subservience, but not integrity. Set against the money nexus is what might be called the genteel poverty one, embracing Mrs Cadwallader, who is obliged to 'get her coals by stratagem' and Mr Farebrother, whose whist-playing for money and occasional sorties to the 'Green Dragon' keep him in moths. Fred feels the pinch but ultimately embraces the work-ethic of the Garths, another important section of the community, where pride in the allotted task takes on the form of dedication and duty.

Lydgate represents the new professional man, as we have seen, having ideals and an enlightened attitude which threatens the existing practitioners who wish their own traditions (and therefore their malpractices) to continue. He too is caught in the money trap, in this instance through marriage, but more offensively in the trap of gossip. One of the salient features in George Eliot's depiction of the narrowness of provincial society is the amount of gossip which is generated as commentary on the main lives, from Mrs Cadwallader's astringent diminishing of Casaubon to the widespread lower level condemnation of Lydgate and Bulstrode without proof.

W. J. Harvey elevates this element somewhat when he says that 'Local politics pervade all aspects of Middlemarch life. But we are never allowed to forget that this provincial story is contained within the broad sweep of national history.' Perhaps not, but one of the ironies of the presentation lies in the fact that *most* of the characters are unaware of that broad sweep or, if they are distantly aware, interpret it with subjective blindness to any issues beyond the local. And the local issues are, to name a few, a young naïve girl getting engaged to a moribund pedant, a decadent landowner buying a newspaper, employing a foreigner, and thinking of standing for Parliament, a new doctor antagonising his colleagues, a banker suspected of murder, and a resentment of the surveyors who come to test the land for the new railway.

The social mores of *Middlemarch* also embrace the clergy, certainly with George Eliot's encompassing irony. Casaubon is the leisured cleric whose attention to doctrine (despite his able pamphlet on the Catholic question) is minimal compared with his absorption in the mythologies. His forgiveness of Dorothea has a distant rectitude which is far from Christian charity. Cadwallader is a balanced and cultured man, but his definition of himself as the 'fishing incumbent' sufficiently indicates his own interests, which could hardly be defined as spiritual. He is, of course, gentry like Casaubon but, unlike the latter, cannot afford a curate, even poorly paid, to do his pastoral work.

The third clergyman is Camden Farebrother, who has the honesty to admit to Lydgate early on that he doubts whether the ministry is his true vocation. Not having the fervour of the apostolic Mr Tyke or the favour of Bulstrode (who ironically considers him a hypocrite) Farebrother does not get the chaplaincy, but he does get the Lowick living in the gift of Dorothea. Experience has made Dorothea clearer-sighted, and she sees the true worth of the man. Farebrother himself tests Fred about taking orders, Mary being the true index to Christian feeling and sincerity in her determination to reject Fred if he becomes a clergyman. Farebrother has much of his author's approval, and his Christianity is seen within his domestic circle, his genuine concern for Lydgate, and his self-sacrifice over Mary. Religion and local politics are, of course, linked in *Middlemarch* through the Tyke affair, but just as Fred is deemed unsuitable for the ministry, so Bulstrode, assertive in his righteousness, is exposed as a hypocrite. Religion for George Eliot is morality, work, duty; becoming a member of the clergy is a profession or an inheritance often having little connection with faith.

4 TECHNICAL FEATURES

4.1 CHARACTERISATION

George Eliot is often referred to as the first modern novelist, for she describes her characters both inwardly and outwardly, as well as commenting omnisciently on their decisions and dilemmas. Her modernity consists in the examination and exposure of the individual consciousness, in integrating her major characters – and most of her minor – psychologically, and in showing consistency, change, development and conditioning through their social, moral and sometimes spiritual environments.

The conventions of the Victorian period forced her to be reticent about sexual matters, but *Middlemarch* effectively demonstrates how imaginative reticence can circumvent convention; I am referring here, for example, to the tomb and taper imagery associated with Casaubon which points to his impotence, and the flower imagery used of Rosamond which stimulates Lydgate's sexual passion. Flowers open to the sun, and Rosamond's forget-me-not blue eyes, bathed in tears, awaken Lydgate's sexual susceptibilities. George Eliot subtly portrays many recognisable human traits, and the majority of her fictional characters are fully rounded and realistically developed.

Dorothea

Dorothea is the central character of *Middlemarch*, the Prelude deliberately drawing the parallel with St Theresa of Avila and investing her with those spiritual and idealistic qualities which we come to recognise so fully in the fictional Dorothea. Yet Dorothea is initially presented with some degree of irony; as the education of her feelings through life experience begins, so the irony diminishes and the compassion with which she is seen deepens. The early chapters show the unworldly Dorothea as idealistic but blind, easily reverencing Mr Casaubon for what she thinks she sees, intent on serving him as if he were, to use George Eliot's analogy, a Protestant Pope. She is blind to the fact that Sir James Chettam's attentions are to her and not, as she thinks, to Celia. She can be proud and haughty, as in her exchanges with Celia over their mother's jewels and her sarcasm over the Maltese terrier to Sir James.

She can also be repentant and childlike, but there are subtle indications of her unawakened nature. Her real vulnerability is in regard to Casaubon; she is so inexperienced that she thinks of him as 'a modern Augustine who united the glories of doctor and saint'.

Dorothea creates her own illusions about Casaubon, believing that she can count on 'understanding, sympathy, and guidance'. She has early warning that he is not interested in the building of cottages for labourers, but her adulation is such that she ignores it. The irony acts as forecast, as she holds up her 'powerful, feminine, maternal hands' before her childless marriage to Casaubon, is obstinately determined to accept him and, when he does propose, in a letter of pedantic and chillingly impersonal devotion, she 'fell on her knees, buried her face, and sobbed'. Her reply is naïve, simply sad in the sense that she uses the word 'devotedly' as the measure of her feeling, which we could perhaps describe as being one of intellectual and spiritual infatuation.

She reacts strongly to Celia's criticisms of the man to whom she has become engaged, and it must be said that the major gap in Dorothea's character throughout the novel is seen in her having no sense of humour at all. But devotion cannot eliminate Dorothea's impulsive emotionalism, and her admission that the great organ at Freiberg made her sob is a telling index to the susceptibility of her nature.

The visit to Lowick prior to her marriage deepens Dorothea's illusions, but she has the practical sense to realise that there seems to be nothing for her to do there. Her first meeting with Will is unpropitious, since she reveals – and it is indicative of the narrowness of her education – an indifference to art. The first hint of the positive dislocation to come occurs when Casaubon expresses the wish that Dorothea should have a companion in Rome on their honeymoon. She is initially haughty in reply, then irritated with herself, then recovers her equanimity, so much so that she always appears outwardly at repose. Her manner is unselfconscious, but Lydgate, on his first meeting with her, finds her 'a little too earnest'. It is an important stress-mark of her character; we might qualify it by saying that Dorothea is a little too earnest for her own good.

Dorothea is next seen in Rome, where the artist Naumann views her as a sort of Christian Antigone – sensuous force controlled by spiritual passion' (chapter 19). Again, the remark is a telling one, for Dorothea is unable to exert 'sensuous force' (she'd renounce it anyway) and her 'spiritual passion' is largely devoted to sterile ends.

The conflicting influence of two civilisations exactly mirrors the conflict within Dorothea – the wish to give and to receive affection, the wish to be ardent and to learn, set against the pedantic pronouncements and the reticent nature of an obviously impotent husband. Dorothea's frustration is made worse by the fact that she is denied entry into her husband's work. Casaubon, threatened, calls forth indignation and resentment from her.

Her attitude towards Will in Rome is one of unmixed openness, goodwill and sincerity, and she admits her limitations – particularly in her appreciation of art – with a winning and naive modesty. She is quick to take offence on her husband's account. Her resilience is shown in her happiness that Casaubon is to be painted as St Thomas Aquinas, her blindness in her second reception of Will, since she is unaware of her husband's disapproval, and her soft-centred idealism in her statement to Will that 'I should like to make life beautiful – I mean everybody's life.' Her sense of gratitude to Will for being so concerned about her shows how innocent and trusting she is. Yet she is not cloying; she is not too good to be true, rather she is too true to be effectively good. She has no idea of tact or judgement in her relations, particularly with her husband.

The return to Lowick is accompanied by the symbolic representation that everything looks smaller, for Dorothea's visions of wifely devotion and duty have shrunk too. She feels a kinship for Ladislaw's grandmother, whose portrait gives her a 'pleasant glow', receives her sister's news of her engagement to Chettam with anxiety (in part attributable to her own marital experiences) and then, after a further disagreement with Casaubon, finds the latter ill.

With her husband's illness Dorothea's life takes on a new phase; she is dependent on Lydgate's advice, and is deeply moved by her husband's suffering. The authorial irony still plays over Dorothea's intense seriousness; we are told that she watches Peter Featherstone's funeral 'with the interest of a monk on his holiday tour' (chapter 34). This is soon broken in upon by the consciousness of Ladislaw's presence and her husband's certain interpretation of it as being her responsibility.

When Will comes to Lowick Dorothea feels a kind of freedom – innocent freedom – from constraint, for she can now 'speak without fear to the one person whom she had found receptive' (chapter 37). Her impulsive, generous, warm nature, as well as her own needs, lead her to say to Will, 'I should like you to stay very much', but she is soon feeling embarrassment and guilt at what her husband's reaction may be. In a moving way this shows how far Dorothea has come; marriage for her, as for anybody, involves an education of the feelings, thought for another, consciousness of action and its consequences. Here the consequences when she tells Casaubon of Will's intention are silence and negation of sympathy; for Dorothea is so out of touch with her husband's feelings that she is 'innocently at work towards the further embitterment' of them. Her suggestion that Will should have money provided for him is salt rubbed into Mr Casaubon's jealous wounds. It is part of the subtlety of her presentation that we should see her not, like Rosamond, egocentric, but simply unable to penetrate the layers of another mind. Although we sympathise with Dorothea we are aware of serious shortcomings, and this makes her a rounded and convincing character.

She always has a 'characteristic directness', and this leads to her telling Mr Brooke how delighted she is that he is to become a reforming landlord under the tutelage of Caleb Garth. Again we note the lack of tact, the transparent honesty. Her idealism has practical and local roots – she speaks uncompromisingly of altering 'the evils which lie under our own hands' (chapter 39). The evil that lies in her own marriage is apparently irremediable, and she is 'much moved' when she learns that Casaubon has forbidden Will to visit him.

With Lydgate's next visit to her husband, Dorothea, intent on showing her husband how much she is concerned for him, takes his arm, which is rigid; when Dorothea is on her own she feels – and this shows the spirit and the passion within her – 'the reaction of a rebellious anger stronger than any she had felt since her marriage' (chapter 42). Yet the comment that follows this experience again elevates Dorothea – 'In such a crisis as this, some women begin to hate.' Despite the struggle, Dorothea doesn't begin to hate. She looks at her husband beseechingly when he eventually comes to bed, and his 'kind, quiet melancholy' stills her reproach. She learns genuine humility from his sympathetic response.

Dorothea's own response to finding Will at Rosamond's – a kind of unarticulated jealousy – soon gives way under Lydgate's appeal to her on behalf of the hospital. Here at last is an outlet for practical activity. But Will's impetuous visit to Lowick Church causes her great embarrassment and 'a look of agitation, as if she were repressing tears', largely because of her husband's determination not to speak to Will or even acknowledge him; yet she still devotes herself unswervingly to Casaubon, reading to him in the night as he moves for once in his life swiftly over his material. But her worst moment is at hand and, faced with Casaubon's wish that she should carry on his work should he die, she delays; she is clear-sighted enough here to see the futility of such a promise and the bleak and arid existence for her should she try to carry it out. Death intervenes, but Dorothea in her hysteria afterwards is so riddled with guilt that she tells Lydgate that 'I am ready to promise'.

It is left to Celia to reveal the truth about Casaubon's will. The 'sobering dose of fact' shows Dorothea how little she knows herself; the 'sudden revelation' brings with it 'a sudden strange yearning of the heart towards Will Ladislaw', the nearest Dorothea can get to an awareness of her own love. She is soon aware, however, that her husband's 'hidden alienation of secrecy and suspicion' and her own 'painful subjection' have diminished him, and she turns quickly to practical matters, notably the chaplaincy question. She is moved to rescue Mr Farebrother from his 'chance-gotten money' by consulting Lydgate, but the latter draws an endearing picture of Will with Henrietta Noble which causes Dorothea to think him 'a creature who entered into every one's feelings'. She also worries about whether he has heard about Casaubon's will.

Dorothea reveals her obstinacy and her independence in determining to return to Lowick. Her individuality and the unique sensitivity and sense of responsibility are seen in the note she writes to her dead husband saying that she cannot carry on with his work. Her longing for Will at first causes her personal embarrassment when he comes to say goodbye, but her genuineness and 'delighted confidence' are soon undermined when she feels that he knows about the will. Their exchange tells us more of Dorothea, for she suffers inwardly throughout, rousing herself to dignity when Sir James Chettam appears, conscious of the fact that he is deprecating Will.

There is a romantic streak in Dorothea, pathetic and unrealised, which makes her treasure the miniature of Will's grandmother and sublimate her grief at being separated from him. Still she has her impetuous and blind moments, symbolically freeing herself by removing her widow's cap, but telling Celia that she will never marry. The individual focus on Dorothea contracts, almost, and this again is subtle, like the contraction of her own life in what Will earlier called the prison of Lowick.

The depth of her feelings for Will is demonstrated when she listens to Mrs Cadwallader's gossip about him 'making a sad dark-blue scandal by warbling continually with your Mr Lydgate's wife'. She is moved, angry, resentful. She feels that there is no 'place for her trustfulness', but when Will comes to say a final goodbye, she still lacks the capacity to release those feelings which make a declaration of love from him possible. But at least when he has gone she knows that he loves her. This knowledge gives her strength and joy despite their parting.

Dorothea speaks the final words of Book VII, a moving and noble declaration of faith in Lydgate: 'You don't believe that Mr Lydgate is guilty of anything base? I will not believe it. Let us find out the truth and clear him!' (chapter 71). Dorothea's moral motivation is always right, but it causes concern among her friends because she is obdurate in pursuing it. Here convention does not stand in her way – her generous belief in others requiring of her a duteous application to their needs. Farebrother, Chettam and, of course, Mr Brooke combine to forestall her action with regard to Lydgate, and she sheds angry tears. But she is determined and sends for Lydgate to come to Lowick.

From now on Dorothea's life revolves around a series of decisions, dilemmas and crises; it is a tribute to her moral strength and stamina that she deals with each one with a generosity of purpose, not a cloying goodness, which makes her real. These are the experiences which, taken with her anguished conditioning in her marriage to Casaubon, finally establish her moral perspective and her capacity for love. She speaks 'fearlessly' to Lydgate of her belief in him, offers him hope, sympathy, faith. There is nobility in her own assertion that people would believe her belief in Lydgate since 'I could have no other motive than truth and justice. I would take any pains to clear you. I have very little to do.'

The pathos of the last sentence is an unselfpitying indication of her own deprivation. With exquisite sympathy Dorothea, a muted idealist herself, responds to the failed idealism of Lydgate. He finds her 'childlike' but 'irresistible', unaware that when he touches on his marriage he is also touching Dorothea's deep suffering in her own. Her response – her suggestion that she should visit Rosamond, and her writing out the cheque for Lydgate when he has gone – show that capacity for altruistic and positive action on behalf of others, which makes us grow in warmth towards her. Dorothea has moved from blindness and pain to insight and joy in giving. Her decisions are based on what is essentially good and right.

Her simplicity, her wish to make a friend of Rosamond, receives a check when she sees Will with her. With wonderful resilience she feels the need for activity on Lydgate's behalf, exulting in 'this triumphant power of indignation', but the inevitable reaction comes. Henrietta Noble's devotion to Ladislaw moves her again; she finds her 'heart was palpitating violently'. Her 'Oh, I did love him!' expresses her doubt in Will, her alternating belief in him, her movement through the night of terrible suffering in her love, through to her looking out of the window in the morning and feeling 'the largeness of the world' and the attendant needs of others than herself. She asks Tantripp for her new dress and bonnet, symbolising her new resolve to conquer her own feelings. With courage, with her self subdued, she makes her 'second attempt to see and save Rosamond' (chapter 80).

That second attempt, the coming together of two totally different women in the intimacy of suffering and understanding, is one of the finest and most moving sequences in *Middlemarch*. Dorothea gives, Rosamond responds by giving and clearing Will, and Dorothea 'could only perceive that this would be joy when she had recovered her power of feeling it'. She comes of age emotionally in this unforced articulation of deep concern and determined self-denial on behalf of Rosamond; her reward is the arousing of a like if temporary generosity in the self-pitying and vain egoist before her.

Dorothea's emotional capacity is here stretched, but the utmost is to come. Aware of her deep love, it is she who at last transcends convention; Will's bitterness, frustration, anger, his exasperated 'Goodbye' release 'the flood of her young passion' and she tells him 'I don't mind about poverty – I hate my wealth' (chapter 83). They are decisive words; love, integrity, truth to the deep needs of her inner self – and Will's – have ensured their future. Her strength against the narrow adversity of Sir James holds up – just as it did over Casaubon – and there is even a touch, rare enough – of humour in her treatment of Celia's concern over the marriage.

The Finale is a moving exposition of her small but 'beneficent activity', her effect on those she comes into contact with being 'incalculably diffusive'. Dorothea is a noble character who has been even more greatly ennobled by suffering. In spite of all that suffering Dorothea is unscarred; there is no reduction in her acceptance, her embracing of simple domesticity, for her happiness will give happiness to others.

Casaubon

Casaubon is pedantic, pompous, sententious – he fits Dorothea in that he is singularly lacking in a sense of humour – impotent both physically and mentally in terms of ever finishing that ambitious project of the Key to all Mythologies. His utterances are carefully weighed, never spontaneous, often appropriately furnished with quotations, his letter of proposal to Dorothea being an index to his nature – dull, arid, lifeless. To Sir James Chettam this man approaching fifty is a 'mummy', while Mrs Cadwallader's phosphorescent tongue calls him 'A great bladder for dried peas to rattle in'.

He does his duty by Will, but has no conception of the vagaries of youth, or even of its needs, as he shows when he describes what is thought of as being great art in Rome, but without the warmth which informs enthusiasm for a subject, an experience or, above all, a relationship. His own imagery of himself – 'My mind is something like the ghost of an ancient' (chapter 2) is revealing. He is a ghost of a man, jealous and withdrawn, insecure enough to feel that Dorothea is prying rather than trying to help, jealous that she may turn to Ladislaw when he dies and that Ladislaw will use her for her money and property. All this shows a nature lacking in human generosity of spirit, for he seeks to rule beyond the grave and will admit no real intimacy this side of it.

Yet it would be unfair to Casaubon – and George Eliot makes this very clear when she says in chapter 29 'but why always Dorothea?' – to stigmatise him merely as a dried-up bookworm. His expectations of marriage are as great as Dorothea's – he stresses his loneliness, his need for companionship – seeing it as restful and quietly rewarding in terms of saving his own eyes. His set habits cannot admit of intrusion. But he has what George Eliot calls 'an intense consciousness within him', and the subtlety and sympathy of his presentation lies in the fact that it is revealed to us.

Casaubon is a pathetic figure, in part aware of his own failure; his self-deception adds to that pathos, since he pretends, even believes, that his thoroughness in research will compensate him for the passing criticism and achievements of others. But he is greatly moved by the awakening knowledge that he and Dorothea are incompatible. She has youth and resilience on her side, Casaubon the startled awareness of suddenly being undermined after a lifetime of self-protection against that outside world which, he often feels, would seek to diminish him. His controlled coldness is replaced by nervousness, and after one angry exchange with Dorothea 'his hand trembled so much that the words seemed to be written in an unknown character' (chapter 29). Shortly after this he has his first attack, contemplates the arrival of 'my second childhood' (chapter 30) and, his sensitivity and possessiveness heightened by his state, immediately suspects Dorothea of collusion in Will's appearance in Middlemarch at Peter Featherstone's funeral.

It tightens his resolve to safeguard her beyond the grave and to tie her to the completion of his work – both the actions of a sick man in the emotional and physical sense. He writes to Will excluding him from Lowick, has his suspicions further increased by Dorothea's wish to make some provision for Will at the present time, and, further driven in upon himself, consults Lydgate. There is some justification for his action when he learns that Will intends to stay in the neighbourhood, for he is now distrustful of everybody.

His inward colloquy (chapter 42) is an admirable summary of his feelings and reactions, cleverly put as a monologue of his hopes and the pressures he now finds upon him. His consultation with Lydgate involves an initial overcoming of his 'proud reticence'. There is a certain courage in his action, though he 'winced perceptibly' when Lydgate tells him of the uncertainty. There is something of the death wish in his reaction too.

He rejects Dorothea's sympathy and then, in a moment of sublime compassion, acknowledges it by his kindness when she sits up waiting for him. But seeing Will at church hardens his resolve; 'the petty anxieties of self-assertion' show him quickly covering his material so that Dorothea may carry on his work. 'The Dead Hand' reaches beyond the grave but has no grip on the ultimate coming together of Dorothea and Will.

Will Ladislaw

The imagery of the sun and light attendant upon Ladislaw has already been referred to. He is somewhat like his predecessor Felix Holt, who suffered from a surfeit of radicalism and authorial approbation. Ladislaw certainly suffers from the latter, but he also suffers from impetuosity, anger, a degree of pride and arrogance, an independence of stance which is somehow not based on substance. He is romantic, poetic, artistic, political (though in exactly what way is never really indicated), irresponsible, charming (when in the mood), kind-hearted, sensitive, tactless and something of a dilettante. All this would be positive if he were fully realised, but he is not a successfully integrated character. His first appearance at Lowick is unpropitious; he colours 'perhaps with temper rather than modesty' (chapter 9) and his sense of humour (singularly lacking on most other occasions) is stirred by the thought of Casaubon as Dorothea's lover, by Brooke's attitude towards his art, but the comment that 'it was the pure enjoyment of comicality' carries little weight. Background integration is undertaken in the next chapter, but Will's deliberate cultivation of excesses and his rejection of them is given to the reader as *past* experience at second-hand.

Will in Rome plays a positive role; he is irritated by Naumann's intention to paint Dorothea. When he visits her he is shy, responds sensitively to the signs that she has been weeping, but inwardly indulges his own hyperbole about the marriage. He gives an 'annihilating pinch' at Casaubon's lack of German, and this again reflects his unthinking impetuosity, since the pinch hurts Dorothea and is an index to his own jealousy. Incurably romantic as well as hyperbolical, he thinks in such terms as 'She was an angel beguiled' while he also waits for the 'melodious fragments in which her heart and soul came forth' (he has already compared her voice to that of an Aeolian harp). George Eliot's description of him includes the phrase 'the little ripple in his nose was a preparation for metamorphosis'. All this militates against realistic presentation.

So intent is he on being with Dorothea that he ingratiates himself with Casaubon, and the painting which Naumann so wishes for is undertaken. Will, it must be allowed, is somewhat humanised by this piece of hypocrisy (he is not all good, far from it) and by his covertly satirical view of the painting, which includes Casaubon. Yet he is irritable and considers

Naumann presumptuous when he mentions Dorothea. His own creed is perhaps best expressed in his own words – 'The best piety is to enjoy – when you can' (chapter 22) – and his now familiar hyperbole embraces Dorothea in her future imprisonment at Lowick. It is human to want to be liked; feeling that he is not liked by Dorothea, Will looked 'dull, not to say sulky'.

Moved by his need to be near Dorothea, Will accepts the editorship of the 'Pioneer' and an unlikely alliance with Mr Brooke, resolutely choosing a course which he knows will offend Casaubon, but Will comes to Lowick to get Dorothea's approbation for his staying too. Dorothea, in her integrity, gives it freely, but we can't help feeling that she has been inveigled into it by her simple trust. Will self-consciously asserts that he loves what is good and beautiful, but he is equally self-conscious about being a rebel. He collects small ragamuffin children and the adoration of Henrietta Noble. Although it is nominally Mr Brooke who is patronising him, in effect Will knows that his 'literary refinements' are too good for Middlemarch and the 'Pioneer'. It is almost as if at times the character we are meant to see as so good through his actions is in fact distanced from us because his eccentricity is so unconvincing. Will is not weak, he is casually opportunist; we are always aware of the stance but never of the person. In the exchanges with Dorothea we feel her anguish and the pettiness of Will's responses despite an authorial focus on his consciousness which never surfaces into life. After the revelations from Bulstrode, after his severance from Brooke, after he learns of Casaubon's will, after his angry recriminations to Rosamond when *he* had put himself in the situation which Dorothea sees, after all that we have been told about him, he is still unable to articulate his love.

Ladislaw is a partial failure of the creative imagination; he does not represent flesh and blood, but ideals and a kind of loose radicalism which provides him with a career at the end. Heathcliff in Emily Brontë's *Wuthering Heights* gnashes, and so does Will; but whereas Heathcliff is recognisably and primitively human in his emotional reflexes, Ladislaw is unrecognisably predictable in his statements and responses. He shows facets of personality without fullness. His author's eye is always upon him. When he raises Dorothea's hand to his lips 'with something like a sob' we are told that 'he stood with his hat and gloves in the other hand, and might have done for the portrait of a Royalist' (chapter 83). It is a telling comment, for the 'radical' is paying his homage to the queen of his romance. Will's mixed lineage might make the remark ironic, but it seems more likely that it is intended to elevate his stature. It is too late, and although his moving expression of love for Dorothea stresses his poverty, we are aware of a different kind of poverty. It is a poverty of being, an insubstantial amalgam of characteristics which do not add up to credibility of character. Ladislaw has had his defenders, but it is difficult to place him in the same category as those characters in the novel who are given realistic and coherent psychological consistency.

Lydgate

Lydgate is one of the triumphs of *Middlemarch* and, with Bulstrode, perhaps the most finely drawn of the male characters in the novel. His 'spots of commonness', his essential susceptibility, his becoming subordinate to Rosamond, the pressures which make him accept the £1000 from Bulstrode, are all drawn with a sure insight into consciousness and motive. An outsider to Middlemarch, he is the object of gossip, speculation and resentment from the other practitioners of the town.

There are obvious and stressed parallels between himself and Dorothea – both are idealists, both choose the wrong way of giving some substance to their idealism, and both strive to overcome petty hindrances in order to achieve their aims. Lydgate has the dubious advantage of being a gentleman by definition and, like Dorothea, an authorial irony is present as the early states of his absorption into Middlemarch are described – 'He said "I think so" with so much deference accompanying the insight of agreement . . .' (chapter 10). The retrospect on Lydgate is effective because it ensures his psychological integration as a character; infatuated with Laure, he finds himself mistaken in his judgement of her, and this capacity for error is to be magnified in his assessment of Rosamond. He is 'young, poor, ambitious' (chapter 11) and thinks that women should look at things from 'the proper feminine angle'.

Lydgate's first meeting with Rosamond exposes his vulnerability; he turns paler when he retrieves her whip. Although he has a 'fearless expectation of success' (chapter 13) he has no sense of the obstacles, social, professional or financial, which he may have to face. He is not lacking in courage, and throws in his lot with Bulstrode over the hospital and the chaplaincy knowing that he will incur hostility. The account of his studying medicine and his determination to advance that study are both finely done, but there is again an indication of his vulnerability expressed with quiet irony in the statement that 'He cared not only for "cases", but for John and Elizabeth, especially Elizabeth' (chapter 15). He chooses the provincial town rather than London, feeling that he will be all the freer from constraint so that he can follow out his own lines of investigation and develop his individual discoveries. His reformist zeal is shown in his refusal to take a percentage on any prescription for drugs, but his main aim is 'to do small work for Middlemarch, and great work for the world' (chapter 15).

After the Laure incident he is determined to take 'a strictly scientific view of woman' (chapter 15). Yet he succumbs immediately to Rosamond (though not in his own mind), lightly employing the birds and bears imagery which accompanies what is courtship to her and, at first, fascinating flirtation for him. Lydgate is already caught up, however, in a wider web, to use the imagery of the novel. He likes Farebrother, but votes for Tyke. He feels that there is 'a pitiable infirmity of will in Mr Farebrother' (chapter 18) without realising that the phrase exactly defines his own frailty.

That frailty is in abeyance while Lydgate makes something of a reputation, correctly diagnosing Fred's illness and treating Casaubon. This breeds both advantage and jealousy. He sits with Rosamond whenever he can, 'calling himself her captive – meaning, all the while, not to be her captive' (chapter 27). He responds fully to Dorothea's concern for her husband (though he secretly wonders at it), but traps himself with Rosamond. In a scene of subtle duplication George Eliot has Rosamond drop her chain (earlier it had been the whip) which Lydgate retrieves. He puts his arms around her 'gently and protectingly', kisses her tears and (encompassed by George Eliot's irony and economy) 'left the house an engaged man, whose soul was not his own, but the woman's to whom he had bound himself' (chapter 31).

Lydgate takes his position for granted, or, as George Eliot puts it, 'he walked by hereditary habit' and 'personal pride and unreflecting egoism' (chapter 36). He thinks of the freedom he will have to pursue his researches when he is married, feeling that 'he had found perfect womanhood'. He gets credit for curing Mrs Larcher's charwoman and the eminent Mr Borthrop Trumbull, though his fellow doctors boycott the Fever Hospital. He confides his views on Vesalius to Rosamond, emphasises his pride in his profession, but the lack of real correspondence between them finds him 'petting her resignedly' (chapter 45). He argues with Ladislaw basically about the ends justifying the means – his 'alliance' with Bulstrode – but is sensitive enough to realise that he has hurt him by casting doubt on Will's 'alliance' with Mr Brooke. His sensitivity is reflected in his plain-speaking to Casaubon, his common-sense concern for and understanding of Dorothea after her husband's death, and his commending Mr Farebrother to her as a fitting incumbent for Lowick. This shows Lydgate's conscience at work; it is some amends for his past vote for Tyke.

Lydgate's honesty and his plain-speaking mark the beginning of the end of any sympathetic understanding with Rosamond; he calls Captain Lydgate 'a conceited ass' (chapter 58), but Rosamond's snobbery has already undermined him before the loss of her baby. That loss finds him wondering at the 'terrible tenacity' of his wife. He soon has to wonder more immediately about his financial situation; forced to become practical instead of casual, rigidly opposed by Rosamond on small and great economies, he dreads the disclosures he must make. He throws himself into his (unpaid) work at the Fever Hospital, cannot bear Farebrother's delicate offer of help, is circumvented by Rosamond in his attempts to get Plymdale to take their house, and, worse, has to endure his uncle's letter as a result of Rosamond's intervention. She has certainly 'mastered him' (chapter 65).

Lydgate's human rewards at the hospital and in private houses cannot compensate him for Rosamond's attitude. Farebrother suspects him of taking opium, and he once gambles at the 'Green Dragon', both marks of his moral decline. His first appeal to Bulstrode for a loan is turned down, but he accepts the latter's cheque unthinkingly when he is called in to attend Raffles, believing that Bulstrode has merely had a change of heart. He is soon made uneasy by Raffles's death, but chooses to doubt his own judgement rather than accuse Bulstrode. Yet another of the 'spots of commonness' has been revealed.

But when Bulstrode is attacked in public at the meeting, Lydgate shows – despite his dislike of what he has to do – that he is not afraid to observe the code of his profession, and he helps the sick man from the room. He is kind to Mrs Bulstrode, but finds himself raging and cursing at himself for ever having come to Middlemarch. He knows his own conscience will stand the test against his fellow doctors, but not against the tainted gossip of the town. He is embittered, in a state of despair, for all Rosamond can urge is that they should leave the town. His own warm and loving nature craves that she should say that she believes in him.

But 'the first assurance of belief in him' (chapter 76) comes from Dorothea, and he finds 'room for the full meaning of his grief'. He confides in her – unaware of the irony for her – about his marriage, is moved by her proposal to see Rosamond, even more moved by the offer of the cheque, but still feels the constraints upon him in trying to follow out his ideals. After Dorothea's visit he feels grateful for Rosamond's 'little mark of interest in him' (chapter 81). Lydgate dies at fifty, having become 'what is called a successful man' though 'he always regarded himself as a failure' and Rosamond as 'his basil plant' (Finale). He carries our sympathies despite his weaknesses; his idealism, unlike Dorothea's, is not transmuted into domestic happiness and localised good works, since his wife has determined on prosperity for Lydgate and herself.

Rosamond

Rosamond is the most complete female egoist in George Eliot's fiction. The authorial irony encapsulates her unlovingly, but Rosamond suffers through her marriage to Lydgate and, although she has a rigid, unchangeable character, there are moments when our sympathies go out to her. Early in the novel's action we find her the mistress of propriety; she is pretty, reasonably talented, says and does the right things, and has certainly a fixed idea that she is always right. She never swerves from this. In chapter 11 we are told that she had that 'nymph-like figure and pure blondness' as well as a 'musical execution' which 'was quite exceptional'.

She boasts that she never speaks in an 'unladylike way', shows her petty snobbery by criticising Fred's breakfasting on red herrings, and contrives to meet Lydgate by driving out with her brother to Stone Court to see the dying Peter Featherstone. She looks down on her uncle's 'horrible relations' and is contrasted effectively with Mary Garth. Rosamond is always aware of herself, and the image of the mirror is used by George Eliot to point up her vanity, for while she is talking to Mary she is really looking at 'the new view of her neck in the glass' (chapter 12). She obliquely questions Mary about Lydgate and, when the latter arrives and retrieves the whip for her, Rosamond finds that she has got what she subconsciously came for, what 'she took to be a mutual impression, called falling in love'.

Rosamond is refined beyond the level of her family; she is clever 'with that sort of cleverness which catches every tone except the humorous' (chapter 16). She is always self-possessed, but the sexuality of her kittenish movements is qualified by the authorial irony that 'she was a sylph caught young and educated at Mrs Lemon's'. She is preoccupied with Lydgate, noting everything about the outer man and knowing nothing of the inner. That is not necessary to her romance. She practises her music and other accomplishments assiduously, setting for herself her 'own standard of a perfect lady'. She persuades her mother to call in Lydgate to treat Fred, and stays long enough 'to show a pretty anxiety conflicting with her sense of what was becoming' (chapter 26). She manages to establish a 'constant understanding' with Lydgate in the sick-room. This gives way to a kind of shyness between them but, with Fred's recovery, Lydgate visits the house and 'To Rosamond it seemed as if she and Lydgate were as good as engaged' (chapter 27).

Rosamond's first check comes with the little lecture Aunt Bulstrode reads her on Lydgate's poverty, and this is reinforced by Lydgate's own resolution to keep away from Rosamond. He keeps it up for ten days, and then succumbs; when Rosamond drops her chain – from nervousness, not intention – she is as natural as she can ever be. Her tears and her silence, again natural, tell her story; she is expressive of her 'timid happiness' and 'had to make her little confession' (chapter 31). Rosamond has got what she wanted, marriage to an outsider of rank, but she has no idea of her future husband's idealism or of his major preoccupations in life. Before that marriage Rosamond has a domestic battle to fight in the form of her father's reaction to Fred's not being Peter Featherstone's heir. There is no question of her losing; she plays on Lydgate's feelings of love and loyalty and then faces her father with the fact that she and Lydgate will not give up each other. Here we see for the first time what Lydgate is later to call the 'terrible tenacity' of Rosamond.

Meanwhile she occupies herself with speculations about Lydgate's family and, aware of the limitations of her own, looks forward to her husband leaving Middlemarch after some time so that they can escape this embarrassment.

After marriage Rosamond asserts her power on a number of levels, but she also persists in indulging romance and ignoring reality, as in her encouraging the visits of Ladislaw. Rosamond is here guilty of a lack of the propriety she so valued before she was married, but marriage has provided her with an increased status. Her response to Lydgate's account of his idealism and his need to work at his research is, 'But we cannot live like hermits' (chapter 43). She compounds this gross insensitivity to her husband's needs later by saying to him, 'I often wish you had not been a medical man' (chapter 45).

Her obstinacy, her courting of the snobbish 'aroma of rank' supplied by Captain Lydgate, causes her to lose her baby, and this despite a severe remonstrance from her husband earlier. Even then she continues obdurate, being 'mildly certain that the ride had made no difference' (chapter 58).

Instead of responding sympathetically to her husband's wish that they should cut down on expenditure, Rosamond reveals the gulf between them by a chill neutrality, asserting that 'I shall do everything it becomes me to do' (chapter 58). She even returns Lydgate's kiss 'faintly', but it is an unsupportive response.

Rosamond never knows when to leave well alone, and her circumventing of Lydgate over the question of getting Ned Plymdale to take their house – a final degradation in Rosamond's eyes – demonstrates both her strength and her insensitivity, just as it demonstrates the qualities of pride and snobbery indicated above. Learning that Lydgate needs £1000 to free them from debt, and learning nothing from her previous errors, she has the fundamental lack of propriety to write to Sir Godwin Lydgate. When the reply comes to her husband her silence is as telling, as cutting, as impenetrable as her words. She seeks refuge ultimately in self-pity, saying that she wishes she had died with her baby.

Rosamond, always capable of indulging a romance, turns to Will Ladislaw in her need. But before that she has to bear the humiliation of having all her invitations to an evening party turned down. When she learns from her father of the rumours about Lydgate and Bulstrode, she feels 'a sense of justified repugnance towards her husband' (chapter 75). She continues to insist on their leaving Middlemarch, but with the visit from Ladislaw, and Dorothea interrupting them while Will is comforting her, Rosamond has to bear personal vituperation perhaps for the first time in her life. Will's 'poisoned weapons' (chapter 78) and his 'No other woman exists by the side of her' puncture Rosamond's romantic illusion much more effectively than anything Lydgate can do or say.

She is made ill and, more important, vulnerable, when Dorothea, after her own anguish, has the generosity of spirit to return and reassure her of Lydgate's innocence. Rosamond feels 'something like bashful timidity before a superior, in the presence of this self-forgetful ardour' (chapter 81). As their exchange deepens in emotional revelation, Rosamond kisses Dorothea, and tells her that Ladislaw loves her, Dorothea. She is even moved to make a gesture of affection towards her long-suffering husband. But she doesn't change; she has her way, and they leave Middlemarch.

She makes a successful second marriage, and never says 'a word in depreciation' of Dorothea. Rosamond's narrow rule, an uncompromising sense of her own rightness, her cultivation of rank and status without ever having a genuine concern for others, make her a sharp and truthful representation of selfishness, the kind of selfishness which subdues others to its wish, though to the superficial outside world it appears charming and irreproachable. In Rosamond George Eliot gets beneath the surface, which all too often passes for truth.

Bulstrode

If Rosamond is the supreme egoist of *Middlemarch*, Bulstrode is the supreme hypocrite who has spent half a lifetime in buying a place in heaven to make up for his sins in the past. He is an unsympathetic character, though deepening suffering, the revelations of that past and the compassion of his wife bring him within the orbit of our own compassion. We first see him at the dinner party (chapter 10), where his words are few and narrow; he is a banker who came to *Middlemarch* twenty-five years ago and married Mr Vincy's sister, Harriet. He is unpopular in the way that successful men often are unpopular, for his subdued tone is thought to be 'inconsistent with openness' (chapter 13). His encounter with Mr Vincy shows him at first obdurate and then vulnerable where the question of family honour is raised – an ironic emphasis in view of the lost family honour to come.

He turns a 'moral lantern' on people and has 'a deferential bending attitude in listening' (chapter 13). He is fervently Evangelical, very conscious of his own health (about which Lydgate forms an unfavourable opinion) and mindful of medical backwardness in Middlemarch, hence his patronage of Lydgate. He also has another motive, and that is to win Lydgate's support for the candidature of Tyke as the hospital chaplain. His charities are numerous but carefully checked, so that his beneficiaries are conscious that he has some hold over them, for he scrutinises their spiritual lives as collateral for his material loans.

After the election of Tyke, Bulstrode is absent from much of the novel's action until he purchases Stone Court from Joshua Rigg Featherstone. At first Bulstrode concentrates on the New Fever Hospital with Lydgate as its superintendent, and tries to raise contributions for it through his committee. Fifteen months after Peter Featherstone's death he engages Caleb Garth to supervise the management of his estate, and is 'conscious of being in a good spiritual frame and more than usually serene, under the influence of his innocent recreation' (chapter 53).

He even thinks somewhat complacently back to the past, and is then confronted by an unwelcome facet of that past, the sudden reappearance of Raffles. The sunshine he had felt gives way to a 'deathly hue', and next morning Raffles begins that process of blackmail which is to undermine him completely. Bulstrode goes back over that past which he fears will be exposed – his wealth accumulated through the dubious goods received at the pawnbroker's, his marriage to the widow of his benefactor and his concealing from that widow the knowledge that her daughter Sarah Dunkirk (mother of Will) has been found. He bribed another man to keep silence, since the woman would not have married him if she thought that her daughter was alive. He pours out his 'utterances of repentance' in the present, and then tries to make amends to Ladislaw by offering him money which would have been rightfully his. Will summarily rejects the offer and, when he has gone, Bulstrode 'suffered a violent reaction, and wept like a woman'.

Fearing for his own sanity, Bulstrode consults Lydgate. His complete selfishness causes him to reject Lydgate's application for a loan ('you should simply become a bankrupt' (chapter 67). He determines to get rid of Raffles, but receives a further blow when Caleb gives up managing his estate on the strength of what he has heard from the sick Raffles. As Lydgate prescribes treatment for the latter, so temptation presents itself to Bulstrode, just as it did in the past over the pawnbroking business and the concealment of Sarah Dunkirk. He makes the loan to Lydgate, and then allows Mrs Abel to give Raffles the liquor which will ensure his death.

The result is his public disgrace and his private humiliation (chapter 71). He goes to the board meeting carrying the same illusion as he had done when he was riding about Stone Court, feeling that 'he should this morning resume his old position as a man of action and influence in the public affairs of the town'. He is mentally and emotionally brave, but his frame is unequal to the exposure, and he is assisted away by Lydgate. At home he is completely broken, though relieved that his wife has had to learn the news from her brother. When she comes to him to offer him her loving support without recrimination they cry together, knowing that their lives are for ever changed.

There is nothing for him to do but to end his days 'in that sad refuge, the indifference of new faces' (chapter 85). Stricken, and constantly self-questioning, he is 'full of timid care for his wife', and even agrees to Fred's installation at Stone Court on land which Bulstrode now regards as virtually belonging to Harriet. The last words have been said. Bulstrode is a hypocrite, but not a coarse one. His moral 'spots of commonness', his self-righteousness, his austerity, hypochondria, coldness, lack of involvement in human experience, his eye always on the judgement of heaven and his own place there, are sufficient indication of the nature of the man. Yet such is George Eliot's art and her own humanity that we suffer with him. His consciousness is probed, his deceptions revealed, his dilemmas spelled out in a fine and sustained analysis of his spiritual, moral and egoistic inward deliberations. Bulstrode is the embodiment of fallen but suffering man.

Harriet Bulstrode

Bulstrode's wife represents loyalty and sincere Christian response. She is concerned for her family and, when Rosamond has led herself to believe that she and Lydgate are as good as engaged, it is Harriet, motivated by concern and not a little inquisitiveness, who undertakes to find out the truth of Lydgate's feelings. It is in chapter 31 that she shows 'a true sisterly feeling for her brother' by making inquiries about Lydgate's intentions, though it is her friend Mrs Plymdale who promotes these by indicating Rosamond's preference for Lydgate and her dismissal of Ned. With typical directness she goes straight to Rosamond and, by forthright questioning, discovers that Rosamond is not engaged. She 'now felt that she had a serious duty before her', and she visits Lydgate. Her language is unequivocal:

> Where you frequent a house it may militate very much against a girl's making a desirable settlement in life, and prevent her from accepting offers even if they are made. (chapter 31)

Serious-minded Mrs Bulstrode reckons without her niece's undoubted charms, and Lydgate succumbs to Rosamond in the same chapter.

Harriet's greatest moment in the novel (chapter 74) is when she stands by her husband in his disgrace. Before that she has to undergo the 'pathetic affectionateness' of Mrs Plymdale and hear the whole story from her brother, Mr Vincy. Even before she hears it, this good woman has made up her mind; the core of her faith and morality is unshakeable – 'and then, after an instant of scorching shame in which she felt only the eyes of the world, with one leap of her heart she was at his side in mournful but unreproaching fellowship with shame and isolation'. In Chapter 5 of this commentary her reactions are analysed as she contemplates her ruined life. There is an inherent nobility in her which transcends narrow faith and the provincial milieu. She accepts her lot and, to the end, is still trying to help her brother's family. She is greatly moved when she reads Lydgate's letter rejecting her husband's help, but she has the tenacity to ensure that Fred gets the chance to look after Stone Court, where he ultimately lives. Harriet is at the heart of *Middlemarch*, the moral crisis precipitating the generous outflow of feeling and giving to the man who has cherished her, despite his guilty past, and whom she has cherished in that past. His future is her love.

Mr Brooke

It would be difficult to find a more complete contrast to Mrs Bulstrode than Mr Brooke. Many 'motes' fall from this magistrate's mind, since he has a compulsive need to talk and to take any direction which presents itself to him without ever completing the journey. Well-born and comfortably off, Mr Brooke is incurably mean, but ironically contemplates standing as the Reform candidate when his own farms are in need of reform.

He has acted as a responsible ward to his nieces, but is loath to abandon the idea of Dorothea marrying Chettam, since their estates adjoin one another. Fortunately, Celia's marriage to the 'worthy baronet' is full compensation. He has some kindliness, and is genuinely concerned for Dorothea both before her marriage and in her early widowhood. But he is an incurable meddler, writing to Ladislaw, providing him with a job and accommodation in Middlemarch and seeing himself as newspaper owner and politician at one and the same moment. Any decision finds him vacillating, any responsibility finds him inadequate to meet it. Today he would be called a 'name-dropper', since his acquaintances include eminent men of his time. He has 'miscellaneous opinions', is always talking about documents, but he has a rooted obstinacy about changing his ways, and this bodes ill for his political career.

That career never gets beyond the balcony of the 'White Hart'; Mr Brooke's election address is undermined by an extra glass of sherry and reduced by an effigy of himself which collects some of the eggs thrown, but not all of them. Mr Brooke the public man finds the meeting too much for him, just as Mr Brooke the private man finds his half-drunken tenant Dagley too much for him. George Eliot presents him ironically throughout; he is a man of position without substance, impressionable but lacking in commitment. He dissipates his energies on passing attractions and consequently has to shift his ground from time to time as these interests change. He is cultivated without being cultured, for he is always 'going into things'. He never gets beyond the superficial, for he hasn't the self-discipline to do so.

The Garths

Although some critics see **Mary Garth** as the real heroine of *Middlemarch* I intend to treat the Garths as it seems certain George Eliot meant them to be seen, as a family with strong moral principles who subserve the ethic that integrity, honesty, hard work and frankness are the codes by which we should live. Mary is a delightful character, a 'brown patch' beside the infantine blondness of Rosamond, but with a luminous intelligence and clear-sightedness which embrace Rosamond's motives as well as Fred's frailties. Lydgate doesn't even notice her, but her attendance on Peter Featherstone typifies her capacity for sacrifice in the interests of others; Mary has a strong sense of duty, though it costs her dearly, as she has to endure the irritability of Peter Featherstone and, at one terrible moment, the temptation to carry out his instructions over the will. She rejects his bribery, and refuses to act, knowing that her refusal will probably injure Fred.

She dislikes scandal and gossip, though she is not stuffy; Rosamond, unconscious of condenscension, calls her 'sensible and useful' (chapter 12), but she is much more than that. She is aware that Rosamond is quizzing her about Lydgate, and humorously gives her an 'inventory' of him. She defends Fred's refusal to take orders, and although she has what is virtually an offer from Farebrother she remains loyal to Fred despite his failure to redeem Caleb's bill, the debt thus incurred costing her own and her mother's savings. Mary is essentially practical, but she is also well-read, a genuinely cultured girl despite the fact that her family 'live in such a poor way' (chapter 11).

She is plain to those who judge by conventional standards, but Fred has always seen the inner beauty which animates her into compassion, kindliness, concern and humour. She is also vulnerable, and Fred's second visit to Stone Court reveals that she has been crying at Featherstone's treatment of her. She rejects romance and lives in reality. She is resilient, and teases Fred through a number of literary parallels, though she also castigates him for his failure to work and for getting into debt. Yet there is no holier-than-thou attitude. When Fred tells her of the debt she reacts passionately as she thinks of her father's suffering, but when she looks at Fred 'her pity for him surmounted her anger and all her other anxieties' (chapter 25). She responds to Caleb's concern for her over Fred with pride and dignity – though both silently know that if Fred reforms then Mary will have him – and only occasionally does the warmth of her character ring wrongly, as when she says to Peter Featherstone, 'I consider my father and mother the best part of myself, sir' (chapter 25).

Mary has 'a well of affectionate gratitude within her' (chapter 33) as well as plenty of merriment. When the wills are read she has the directness (though with 'affectionate sadness') to tell Fred that he will be better off without the money. With Caleb's advancements Mary is able to stay at home, to the delight of her parents and the children. She is seen greatly to advantage in these domestic interiors. Aware of a slight change in Mr Farebrother's manner towards her, she tells him that she is too fond of Fred to give him up. Even here, though, she responds sympathetically to 'the resolute suppression of a pain in Mr Farebrother's manner' (chapter 52). She marries Fred after he has proved himself under Mr Garth's tutelage, helps him with the running of Stone Court and has three children for whom she writes a book. Mary is wise beyond her years, but she is not cloying; she says what she thinks, but is always vulnerable and sympathetic, warm and involved.

Caleb is of the same equality, and one of the endearing things about the Garths is that George Eliot gives them a family consistency. Caleb has little head for business; rather he is interested in the quality of the work he produces and the challenge that it calls out in him. His integrity has communicated itself to Mary, who inherits it; that integrity consists of straight dealing and an inherent generosity. He unthinkingly gives his bond to Fred (and just as absent-mindedly forgets to tell his wife that he has done so), and makes the best of the misfortune, though he concernedly questions Mary about her feelings for Fred. His intuition and love for her tell him that she cares for Fred.

He appreciates Fred's help over the incident with the farm labourers who are objecting to the railway, but bluntly tells him that he must begin at the bottom if he is to come into his business. He helps him and, with typical care, generosity and genuine liking for Fred, secures the management of Stone Court for him aided, of course, by Harriet Bulstrode. His worth is shown by the fact that Sir James Chettam turns to him for the management of his estates, as does Bulstrode; but typically, after Caleb meets the sick Raffles he tells Bulstrode that he will no longer work for him. His moral stance, and his compassion for the sick man, urge this decision, for Caleb, easy-going over money, is capable of definite action when his own code of morality prescribes it.

Susan Garth complements her husband admirably, and the children, particularly Ben, are among George Eliot's best and most endearing. Susan has a sharper tongue than her husband – she almost uses it when Fred brings his unwelcome news – but she also has his largeness of heart. She teaches as she works, and we see where Mary gets her interest in literature from when we see what a cultured woman Mrs Garth is. She knows that her husband is soft, but she never reproaches him; she loves him for his goodness and supplements it with an integrity and dedication – and warmth – which show the depth of their love. Like her husband, she represents right conduct, but she is too down-to-earth to have any self-righteousness in what she does. For her, life has been a struggle, but always with an accompanying inner happiness in the circle of family love.

The Vincys

Fred's is the most important story among the Vincys (we have already analysed Rosamond's character). He has failed at college, got in with a low racing set which he thinks he enjoys, and always feels that things will turn out all right until the reading of Peter Featherstone's second will. He is also conscious that he could take holy orders and that he has always been in love with a plain girl who is looked down on by his family. He is his mother's favourite and his father's embarrassment. Irresponsible with regard to money, unable to take any firm course of work, Fred appears feckless, yet there is something very attractive about him.

To his great credit he never swerves in his love for Mary, and is made miserable by his own actions when he sees the effect on her. Fred's inherent goodness is shown on a number of occasions; he manages to get Lydgate away from gambling, being embarrassed on Lydgate's own account, and has delicacy of feeling enough to listen to Farebrother's words about himself and Mary, and to realise that Farebrother is generously acknowledging Mary's preference for Fred and asking the latter to be worthy of her. Fred responds with a like generosity, and afterwards ascribes his happiness with Mary to Mr Farebrother. Fred proves to be practical under the tutelage of Mr Garth, and becomes his own man independent of the wishes of his family.

Mrs Vincy dotes on him, but has spoiled him. She is tearful and worried about Fred in his illness, blaming Wrench irrationally for it. She is thoughtless and reacts impetuously, but her husband is of a different calibre. Mr Vincy is worried about financial and trading matters, he has a kind of family pride and a directness though, like his wife, he is impetuous. He goes straight to Bulstrode to get the letter; he reacts angrily when he hears the wills read, and takes it out on Fred when he gets home. He also utters threats against Rosamond's engagement, but much of what he says is impulsive bluster, and Rosamond soon brings him round. Perhaps his most signal sympathetic contribution is to tell Harriet Bulstrode of her husband's past. Vincy has a sense of self-importance, but also of practicality, and does not attempt to stop Fred joining Caleb Garth.

Mr Farebrother

Farebrother is superseded at the hospital by Tyke (he had been doing some of the work of the chaplain unpaid), just as Bulstrode wishes. He is about forty, and 'came like a pleasant change in the light' (chapter 16) when he visits the Vincys and plays whist. In his own home he is somewhat ruled by his mother, and certainly there is a general family wish that he should marry Mary Garth. He shows his own inclinations in this direction with marked delicacy, but defers to her long-standing love for Fred.

He is adored by his 'womankind', has made 'an exhaustive study of the entomology of this district' (chapter 17) and he is honest enough to tell Lydgate that he is not completely happy in his calling. Obviously he uses his minor winnings at cards to buy books and add to his collection.

Despite his small temptations Farebrother is a man of integrity, and is not offended by Lydgate's being Bulstrode's protégé in a sense, though he later warns him about becoming too dependent on Bulstrode. In terms of the space allocated to him in the novel, Farebrother is a minor character, but he is a major moral influence. He disregards 'the Middlemarch discrimination of ranks' (chapter 40) and visits the Garths whenever he feels like it, for he is particularly fond of them. He also visits them on Fred's behalf, to tell them that Fred is going to take his degree, and invites Mary to stay at the Vicarage. For a moment he contemplates the possibility that he might marry, and this is perhaps strengthened when Dorothea gives him the living of Lowick. In advising Fred, Farebrother reveals a degree of self-knowledge which is heart-warming – he is aware that he himself has 'been too lax' (chapter 52). He undertakes on Fred's behalf to talk to Mary, and with his customary delicacy reveals to her that she has not injured Fred by preventing Featherstone from burning the second will. He questions Mary about her feelings, gets the reply he fears, and consciously controls his own inward pain, though Mary is keen enough to see it. Later he even leaves Fred and Mary together so that they can talk, unaware that he has aroused a strong jealousy in Fred's bosom.

Farebrother is himself generally observant though, and notices that Lydgate 'may have been taking an opiate' (chapter 63). He begins to see into Lydgate's marriage and his troubles but, as always, treats his friend with delicacy and reticence, knowing full well that Lydgate is a proud man. But his nobility of character urges him to speak to Fred about the woman they both love. In doing so he gives up Mary to Fred with a free generosity of spirit which Fred at once acknowledges. He thinks the best of Bulstrode for lending Lydgate money, but when the Bulstrode–Lydgate scandal breaks he urges caution on Dorothea, who impetuously wishes to clear Lydgate's name. Farebrother's family are quite delightful, his mother being sharp and devoted to him, as is Miss Winifred, while Henrietta Noble in her absent-minded eccentricities also has an important functional role to play in the plot. We remember that she had said that she would use Ladislaw's shoes as pillows; in fact she initiates his final meeting with Dorothea by telling Dorothea that Will is waiting to see her.

Other Characters

Sir James Chettam, initially the amiable baronet who listens to Dorothea's schemes, plays a strong part in the early chapters. He is disgusted by Dorothea's engagement to Casaubon, and urges on Mr Brooke and Mr Cadwallader the necessity for some action to prevent the marriage. He has been blind to Dorothea's responses to himself, but a hint from Mrs Cadwallader points him in the direction of Celia. He continues, however, to have rather more than a protective attitude towards Dorothea after her marriage, and influences Brooke towards reforms by employing Caleb Garth and urging Mr Brooke to do so.

His marriage is happy, but he has an acute sense of status, and frets unnecessarily about Dorothea learning the provisions of her husband's will. There is a subtle element in the portrayal of Sir James which suggests that he never falls completely out of love with Dorothea; when the latter marries he refuses to meet Ladislaw, and only some time afterwards, when Dorothea has a baby, does Celia manage to bring about the reconciliation, for Sir James beneath his exterior is essentially soft-hearted.

Celia is a telling contrast to Dorothea – clear-sighted, open, a little in awe of the superior accomplishments of her sister, but able to put her down with balanced bluntness. She doesn't spare Dorothea over Casaubon until she actually learns that her sister is engaged; she enlightens Dorothea about Sir James's real preference, is much more concerned with outward appearances than is Dorothea, and quickly assumes her married status and motherhood. After Casaubon's death she nags Dorothea to remove her widow's cap, always showing her solicitude though inclined to let her tongue run away with her. She is affectionate and loving, intent on her child and on Dorothea's participation in its life. She has common sense and, occasionally, a kind of insensitivity, provoking Dorothea both before and after her marriage.

The Cadwalladers serve as a delightful contrast to each other. Mrs Cadwallader, match-maker of the acid tongue and retailer of the latest gossip with splendid periods of witty rhetoric (see the critical commentaries on the chapters in which she appears), is the dominant one of the pair. She pulls no verbal punches, is free in any society and advertises her (comparative) poverty, for we know that she has to get her coals by stratagem. She is strong-minded and powerful in argument, and she is clear-sighted too, as we see when she deals with Sir James after he has over-reacted to Dorothea's engagement. Mr Brooke goes in fear of her verbal missiles for, although she is friendly, she is too sudden and forthright for that vacillating man. Her husband represents balance and moderation, the 'fishing incumbent' acting as an admirable foil to his wife's loquacity. He is sensible both of others and of himself, and has a wry sense of humour which contrasts with his wife's racy fireworks. That sense of irony which characterises Peter Featherstone's treatment of his relatives is sustained after his death in his choice of Mr Cadwallader to conduct his funeral service.

Peter Featherstone almost dominates the chapters in which he appears; we can see from our glimpses of the dying man how he came to make money, for he is cunning, unscrupulous, able to play off one person against another, always getting his own way until he comes up against the moral integrity of Mary Garth in his final moments. His running dismissal of his relations, his humiliation of Fred, his inverted snobbery over Fred as a university man too, plus his petty exercise of authority over Mary, all indicate his love of power. This love extends beyond the grave; the reading of the two wills plus the appearance and casual triumph of Joshua Rigg Featherstone are a tribute to the malicious enjoyment of the old man. That enjoyment consists of hurting and manipulating, and his disinheriting all those who have paid court to him is the final exercise of a sardonic humour; his attempt to change the course of what he has decreed at the last moment has a finely ironic flavour for, as Mr Farebrother tells Mary, the burning of the second will would not have made the first one valid.

It is not my intention here to go through all the minor characters in *Middlemarch*, except to say in passing that realistic strokes bring them quickly and positively to life, as in Dagley and his exchange with Mr Brooke, Mrs Dollop, Mr Hawley (in his indictment of Bulstrode), Dorothea's servant Tantripp, Will's friend Naumann and a living gallery of others. Perhaps two are worth special mention, the one for the quality of the caricature which is close to reality, the other for his functional part in the plot.

I refer to **Borthrop Trumbull** in the first instance. The auctioneer has been called Dickensian, and certainly he would fit in terms of verve and presence; but such is George Eliot's subtlety that we feel a certain sense of deprivation in him too. He notices the competence of Mary Garth, and his established habit of repeating himself and extending what he has to say via a reflex tautology also has something of pathos in it. He is further exposed by his illness; his condescension to Lydgate is replaced by genuine gratitude, and again we feel the loneliness of the man whose only life would appear to be in his public words.

Raffles is caricature, as is Rigg, but he is effective caricature, shedding a grotesque light on Bulstrode's past when we think of what we know of his present. He is the typical blackmailer, always after more and knowing that he will get it. Despite his habits he is still sharp enough to put his mind to work on the Ladislaw–Bulstrode connection. There is a kind of justice in his death.

4.2 STYLE AND STRUCTURE

Introduction

Style and structure are intimately related in *Middlemarch*, growing out of that awareness of total relevance which characterises George Eliot's mature work. There are patterns of imagery which are in effect comments on character and situation, on decision and dilemma. There is a measured use of symbol, that of the pier-glass for example, where the scratches going in all directions reflect Rosamond's egoism and the wide-ranging interaction of individual lives on each other. There is the omniscient control of narrative, and the use of the omniscient voice in moral, elevated or even philosophical comment. There is the use of commentary on character which often comes from within character or from a supposedly neutral perspective. There is the convincing use of dialogue as a natural extension of character in action. There is the contrast and parallel of characters and situations, and there are the chapter mottoes and book titles, the first an often intimate identification with immediate or wider content, the second the major signposts of action and form in the total structure. Frederic Harrison's celebrated comment on the nature of *Felix Holt* – that it merited as much detailed critical reading as *In Memoriam* because of its richness – surely applies more comprehensively to *Middlemarch*. And one must add, since it needs saying, that *Middlemarch* is the work of a learned mind, and the text, like that of T. S. Eliot's *The Waste Land*, is allusive in that learning, which is itself an enrichment and expansion of the text. The main aspects of George Eliot's *style* and their relationship to her sense of *structure* are examined below.

Imagery

Since there has been some indication in chapter 2 of George Eliot's use of imagery and its significance, I merely intend here to indicate certain areas of usage which enhance our understanding of character. Light and the sun are associated with Ladislaw, and there are frequent references to his laugh and his hair as being evocative of the life-giving force. This light imagery is balanced by the 'rayless' descriptions of Casaubon and by the imagery of the tomb and the taper – darkness and flickering light, death and impotence by implication. We should add to the general run of water imagery, almost all used ironically, the comparison of Lydgate to a swimmer in chapter 16. Casaubon finds marriage an 'enclosed basin' and love a 'shallow rill', but Lydgate, who is spoken of as an explorer and a circumnavigator, has attendant imagery which shows, as here, his strength in pursuit of his studies which, alas, is soon to be undermined by lack of money and, above all, the chill influence without intimacy of Rosamond. Water imagery is redolent of life in *Middlemarch*, the life of the mind and the emotions.

Imagery of the maze or labyrinth is used in *Middlemarch* (together with Ladislaw's hyperbolical 'prison' imagery) to indicate the mental impotence and confusion of Casaubon, and it is also used to show that Dorothea's marriage is going nowhere, like the mind of her husband. It contrasts with imagery of the web, central to the novel, which is itself definitive of George Eliot's own narrative concern with total relevance. Imagery of flowers and nature varies considerably in its emphasis; flowers are used with water imagery to ironically define Rosamond's attractiveness – sexual attractiveness – and also her kind of superficial prettiness:

> . . . she felt that her tears had risen, and it was no use trying to do anything else than let them stay like water on a blue flower . . . . Remember that the ambitious man who was looking at those Forget-me-nots under the water was very warm-hearted and rash . . . . (chapter 31)

Almost immediately afterwards George Eliot refers to Rosamond's being able to raise 'the power of passionate love lying buried there in no sealed sepulchre, but under the lightest, easily pierced mould'. I have given this with some fullness because it demonstrates George Eliot's control of mixed imagery as ironic comment, here on the nature of delusion and the effects which are to come from it. The flowers are linked with a death image – the sepulchre – which is itself a unifying image, since it looks across at the death imagery associated with Casaubon. The further analogy is, of course, with marriage, which is a death to the soul and the spirit if there is incompatibility of emotional depth and giving. Dorothea uses a kind of equivalent when she talks to Rosamond of marriage, which 'drinks up all our power of giving or getting any blessedness ... and then the marriage stays with us like a murder' (chapter 81).

There are a range of other images, physical language (like 'wound') being used quite simply as a correlative of emotional pain or injury; animal and bird images, as well as musical images, are all used to emphasise character traits. Barbara Hardy (see Further Reading) has drawn attention to images of disenchantment, the room being a kind of scene which correlates with a character's mood, as when Dorothea returns from her wedding journey to Rome to the room which she had visited before her marriage; then she had seen everything as soberly but ideally tranquil, full of dedication and love. Now it is changed:

> The very furniture in the room seemed to have shrunk since she saw it before; the stag in the tapestry looked more like a ghost in his ghostly blue-green world .... (chapter 28).

Again we are aware of the subtlety; the stag is associated with Casaubon, and the image reflects his impotence, his own 'shrinking' from Dorothea's intimacy, his 'shrinking' too in her mind. But that is not all. The tapestry also sets up a resonance in the reader's mind, for it is connected with the web and the maze, its stitches labyrinthine in extent to indicate the emotional meshes in which Dorothea is caught. The selection of images here has been necessarily brief – for example, we have not looked at representations of Dorothea which stress her childlike qualities, particularly in scenes with Will.

Symbols

Images in the novel often take on the force of symbols, and certainly the mirror and window images and that of the pier-glass come into this category. Certain images have the strength of symbols. Imagery is descriptive language which generally appeals to the senses and is a commentary on character or situation. A symbol – generally an object or idea – is used to stand for something else with which it is associated either explicitly or in some more subtle way. The pier-glass is used at the beginning of chapter 27:

> Your pier-glass or extensive surface of polished steel made to be rubbed by a housemaid, will be minutely and multitudinously scratched in all directions; but place now against it a lighted candle as a centre of illumination, and lo! the scratches will seem to arrange themselves in a fine series of concentric circles round that little sun .... These things are a parable. The scratches are events, and the candle is the egoism of any person now absent – of Miss Vincy, for example.

The symbol conveys not only the perspective of the author and her method, it also conveys the distortion of egoism which is concerned with self. It thus supports, as does the mirror, one of the moral standpoints of the novel, which is that egoism degrades individuality and adversely affects relationships. Barbara Hardy has demonstrated that the mirror image can be used humorously, as when Bulstrode finds that Mr Vincy is one too much for him, and 'had ended by seeing a very unsatisfactory reflection of himself in the coarse unflattering mirror which that manufacturer's mind presented to the subtler lights and shadows of his fellow men' (chapter 13). She also notes that the motto for chapter 72 contains the line 'Full souls are double mirrors', an emphasis on the fact that Dorothea has come through experience (of the single mirror ego of Casaubon) to clear-sightedness, here seen in her appraisal of Lydgate. Rosamond, on her first visit to Peter Featherstone with Fred, is seen in contrast to Mary through the image. They stand near the window, and we see two Rosamonds – 'the one in the glass, and the one out of it' (chapter 12) – i.e. Rosamond as she appears *and* as she is, vain and egocentric. Mary calls herself a 'brown patch' as she sees her own reflection, but Rosamond is conscious of her own potential – and the possible meeting with Lydgate, so that her eyes are 'swerving towards the new view of her neck in the glass'.

But if the mirror symbolises the ego, the window is the escape from self, the looking out into the world beyond. Easily the best example of this is when Dorothea spends her night of hard anguish before the light of the following day. Even here there are additional images before the main symbol is used – the room has 'light piercing into' it (perhaps symbolic of Ladislaw's appearance and his effect on Dorothea), while she thinks of 'rescue' and wishes she could 'clutch my own pain, and compel it to silence' (chapter 80). When she pulls the curtains she looks through the window and beyond the entrance-gates of her 'prison':

> On the road there was a man with a bundle on his back and a woman carrying her baby; in the field she could see figures moving – perhaps the shepherd with his dog. Far off in the bending sky was the pearly light; and she felt the largeness of the world and the manifold wakings of men to labour and endurance. She was a part of that

involuntary, palpitating life, and could neither look out on it from her luxurious shelter as a mere spectator, nor hide her eyes in selfish complaining.

Now this passage is often quoted by critics as a symbol of outward looking, but I intend to show that it is not only that. It is a symbol of the looking outward, and inward, and across, of the novelist herself. It is a brilliant piece of unifying and pre-figuring writing. For example, take the picture of the man, woman and child, and you have the situation of Dorothea and Will as given in the Finale. The figures here symbolise them and their movement out into the world in the future, with the bundle on the man's back being the burden of the codicil which Will has to bear, despite Dorothea's sharing her life with him. The fact that Dorothea can't quite discern the figures moving is significant – her imagination creates them, the shepherd and his dog, symbolic of security, the permanence of man in nature, the settled life she so longs for. The pearly light in the sky symbolises the irradiation which Ladislaw is to bring into her life – note the span of space, contrasted with the small room of her existence – while 'labour and endurance' are key words in *Middlemarch*, the first the work-ethic epitomised by the Garths, the second the suffering which is necessary for the education of the feelings through experience into new awareness.

The spectator image (Rosamond has an audience in her own consciousness) is a cunning self-image, contrasting with the 'palpitating life' which is reality; Bulstrode too is constantly 'watching' himself, while Casaubon showed an unpleasant awareness that others were always watching him, whether Dorothea close at hand or Carp and company at Brasenose. The 'nor hide her eyes in selfish complaining' looks across at Bulstrode and Rosamond, for the first has, so to speak, already hidden his eyes, and Rosamond's 'selfish complaining', though perfectly within the proprieties of Mrs Lemon's, is the assertion of self. Thus the whole paragraph is revelatory of the new Dorothea, has echoes of other characters in the novel, and sets moral participation in life as the pattern. Significantly, Dorothea now chooses a new dress, the symbol of her new involvement in life, just as Harriet Bulstrode chooses a black dress in token of repentance for her husband's past.

Dialogue and description

Like Jane Austen, George Eliot needs very little translation to the television screen. Her dialogue is natural and unforced, and the range is impressive, from the verbal vacillations of Mr Brooke to the drunken invective of his tenant Dagley, from the sing-song pedantry of Casaubon to the vivacious and impulsive ardours of Dorothea. It is true to say that no single character in the novel could be mistaken for any other; all speech is in character and markedly idiosyncratic, as in the inflated periods of Mr Borthrop Trumbull and the aggressive insensitivity of Peter Featherstone. Nowhere is the idiosyncratic more marked than in the strongly satirical views of Mrs Cadwallader or in her bluntness which Mr Brooke finds so disturbing ('People should consume their independent nonsense at home, not hawk it about' – chapter 6), advice which he himself is incapable of taking. Rosamond's propriety is exemplified in her speech, Bulstrode's self-conscious religiosity in his. Mary Garth's humour vitalises her words, particularly to Fred, and Caleb's mildness, his wife's rather sharper incisiveness and even the eccentricities of Henrietta Noble are captured with affectionate but not cloying accuracy.

Description of interiors, particularly that at Lowick, or exteriors, as with Dorothea at Rome, is wonderfully done. We have to turn back to *Adam Bede* and *The Mill on the Floss* for the fullness of natural description, but *Middlemarch* has its share, albeit brief. Much more in the foreground is what I would call atmospheric description, as when Mr Brooke makes his fated electioneering address, where George Eliot captures crowd atmosphere and focuses on the punch-voiced echo of Mr Brooke which soon defeats that unfortunate man. *Middlemarch* has many set pieces of description, notably of Dorothea at the very beginning of the novel, and part of this is deliberately ironic. The infantine blondness of Rosamond draws its share of the irony, and physical description is used to point up character traits, as in the 'deferential bending attitude in listening' (chapter 13) which is prefaced by an account of Bulstrode's 'sickly aspect' and 'pale blond skin, thin grey-besprinkled brown hair, light-grey eyes, and a large forehead'. Much is made of Casaubon's lack of physique and Chettam's abundant health, while the satirical vein is reserved for Mr Borthrop Trumbull.

Contrast and parallel

These have been largely indicated in the commentaries on books and chapters, particularly in terms of character, and will only be given briefly here. Lydgate and Dorothea are idealists who fail; both make unhappy marriages. Rosamond, Bulstrode and Casaubon are studies in egoism; the Garths and Dorothea are studies in altruism, and both are linked with Lydgate through the work-ethic. Dorothea can be contrasted with Rosamond, Caleb Garth with Bulstrode, Mrs Garth with Mrs Vincy, Mr Brooke with Chettam, Dorothea with Celia and so on. Other contrasts, as we have seen from the foregoing chapter, are to be found in the imagery which is related to character or which is a comment on situation.

The pattern of parallel and contrast is shown in the Book headings, for example Book II ('Old and Young'), which deals largely with Dorothea and Casaubon, as well as Peter Featherstone and the aspirations of Fred. Book IV ('Three Love Problems') examines those of Fred and Mary, Dorothea and Casaubon, Rosamond and Lydgate, but by extension Will's own problems of love are beginning to make themselves felt. Book V ('The Dead Hand') has Peter Featherstone's reaching out beyond the grave in the sense that it changes Fred's destiny, but more particularly here we have the effect of Casaubon's will and the dead hand of the past through Raffles being placed on Bulstrode's shoulder, so to speak. Book VI ('The Widow and the Wife') is expressive of the sharpening focus on Dorothea, her widowhood providing her with opportunities to do good though she is contrained by her husband's will. Rosamond is the wife of the title, ironically in name only, but such is the structural coherence of *Middlemarch* that the other wife – Harriet Bulstrode – is already in our minds as her husband's past begins to be revealed. The wife-to-be, Mary Garth, is also present in the background. Book VII ('Two Temptations') brings Lydgate and Bulstrode into interaction, with Bulstrode tempted to dispose of Raffles (via Mrs Abel) and Lydgate tempted to accept his £1000, to which he succumbs, though Dorothea later rescues him from this obligation. Once again, there are more than two temptations; following the ramblings of Raffles, Caleb refuses to continue working for Bulstrode, Lydgate is tempted to gamble, Rosamond is tempted to write to Sir Godwin and does so, Fred is tempted towards the 'Green Dragon' but saves Lydgate.

Nowhere is the multiple structure of *Middlemarch* more in evidence than in Book VIII ('Sunset and Sunrise'), where the antithetical balance serves to emphasise the playing out of certain lives and the emergence into positive relationship of others, the first perhaps epitomised by the fading of Bulstrode and Lydgate in their separate ways, the love of Mary and Fred, Dorothea and Will being the main constituents of the second. I have used the Book titles here to indicate the main areas of structural parallel and contrast, but the interested student will doubtless find others which may be explored on another level. As indicated earlier, the chapter mottoes should be read attentively, since they are integral to the text both in commentary, evaluation and, sometimes, indicative of the structural unity of the novel.

Culture and learning

There is little doubt that George Eliot is one of the most learned and cultured of English novelists. No glossary of references is provided in this study, since it would run into pages, and the two annotated editions referred to in Further Reading provide many notes on the actual text. But no study of *Middlemarch* would be complete without some reference to the *range* of George Eliot's knowledge and the quality of her deployment of it. This is not to say that it is ostentatious; it is centrally part of her conception, giving her novel authority and lending it the kind of distinction which a great work of art possesses. Historical and scientific references have for the most part been covered in chapter 3, but George Eliot's concerns embrace literature, both foreign and English, art, music, other aspects of science, religion, both Christian and Pagan and also other profound areas of knowledge.

The first chapter of *Middlemarch* has for its motto a quotation from Beaumont and Fletcher's *The Maid's Tragedy* which establishes neatly one of the major themes of the novel:

>Since I can do no good because a woman,
>Reach constantly at something that is near it.

We do not need to know the play in question – though, as so often, knowledge of it might even provide a sub-text for a part of *Middlemarch* – for the quotation not only defines Dorothea in a male society, but also, because of its title, anticipates the domestic tragedy of a maid who is to remain a maid in her marriage. Within that first chapter we have references to Dorothea's conditioning in religious terms and accounts of her own need to dedicate herself – for example the mention of Pascal (1623–62) and his *Pensées* (not published until 1670), which are fragments of a Christian apologia, though the Frenchman was also a philosopher, mathematician and physicist. There is also a reference to Dorothea's familiarity with Jeremy Taylor (1613–67), English cleric celebrated for his devotions, the theologian Richard Hooker (1554–1600), who influenced Anglicanism with his *Laws of Ecclesiastical Polity* (1593–97) and John Milton (1608–74), the great English poet and author of *Paradise Lost* (1667; 1674). These are merely examples, but they establish Dorothea's interests, while in the second chapter her blindness is anticipated by a motto from Cervantes' *Don Quixote*. Within that chapter Mr Brooke mentions Sir Humphry Davy's book on *Agricultural Chemistry* (1814), Mr Brooke (since Davy was also a poet) finding a link with Wordsworth (1770–1850), the composite reference indicating the nature of contemporary interests at this time (1829). Thus the learning is both a comment on character and an authentication of period.

Classical references run throughout (including that of the maze or labyrinth referred to earlier); in chapter 6 Mrs Cadwallader refers to 'our Lowick Cicero', an ironic snipe at Casaubon's researches and perhaps at his style too. Cicero (106–43 BC) is regarded as the supreme master of Latin prose. In the same chapter Mr Brooke quotes from the Latin poet Virgil (70–19 BC) and another classical reference is to Sappho, the sixth century BC lyric poetess of Lesbos. Pagan references are sometimes reinforced by Pagan authority, and Casaubon cites Aristotle in support of what Will should do, Will countering by calling himself Pegasus (the immortal winged horse who sprang from the blood of the slain Medusa). The classical reference here provides an effective contrast between the two men merely by the nature of the source they choose. Will's imagination is not fettered to learning, while Casaubon's learning is trapped in allusions which have little or no connection with life. This is one of a number of classical references which repay attention and provide in fact a sub-text to the novel. For example, George Eliot cites Herodotus (485–425 BC), 'who also, in telling what had been, thought it well to take a woman's lot for his starting-point' (chapter 11). Even casual references have Rosamond as a sylph and a nymph, Farebrother speaks of the 'sirens', and Rosamond feels as 'forlorn as Ariadne – as a charming stage Ariadne' (chapter 31). Mrs Vincy is compared to Niobe (chapter 16), Horace's *Ars Poetica* is mentioned in chapter 34, Actaeon and Diana in chapter 43 and Ladislaw is equated with Daphnis (the supposed inventor of pastoral poetry) in chapter 50. The mythological references underpin the realistic narrative; the *Key to All Mythologies* is never to see the daylight.

Literary references, to both English and foreign literature, are also part of the intellectual fabric, the human tapestry, of *Middlemarch*. Mr Brooke, his mind ever wandering, is sometimes inaccurate, ascribing Dr Johnson's:

> ' Let observation with extensive view
> Survey mankind, from China to Peru

to *The Rambler* and not to *The Vanity of Human Wishes*. But George Eliot herself *is* accurate, and the chapter mottoes show her drawing extensively on Shakespeare – both the plays and the sonnets – with a roughly equal mix from tragedies, comedies and histories, perhaps reflected in the subject matter of *Middlemarch* itself. George Eliot's beloved Sir Walter Scott (1771–1832) gets two references in chapter 14, one to *Waverley* (1814), the other to *The Pirate* (1822), but her saturation in his works (which she re-read to her dying father) receives a personal accolade in chapter 57, where a motto-sonnet of her own to Scott is imbued with her childhood memories of the pleasure and excitement he gave her. By way of light relief, Mr Borthrop Trumbull mangles the pronunciation of *Ann of Geierstein* (1829). Pascal's *Pensées*, early associated with Dorothea, gets several mentions, while, in addition to a range of English authors, Dante, Goethe, Racine, Victor Hugo and Musset are also used in mottoes which are commentaries on or extensions of the text. Perhaps the most significant and pertinent English authors referred to are Donne, Blake and Bunyan, though one Spenser sonnet (from *Amoretti*) at the head of chapter 37 ('Thrice happy she that is so well assured/Unto herself . . .') glances directly at the egocentricity of Rosamond.

References to art and music are also central to *Middlemarch*, with Dorothea's experiences in Rome set against the background of Will's own interests in art – he is a kind of pre-Raphaelite himself – and Naumann's obvious allegiance to the Nazarene school of art, whose disciples were in fact the pre-Raphaelites in England. Art and sculpture are much in evidence in chapters 19 to 22, while music is actually used as an index to depth of character, particularly with regard to Rosamond and Dorothea. The former sings songs like 'Home sweet home', though in all fairness one must say that she detested it; Dorothea sobs at the music of the great organ in Freiberg, Will composes his own ballad as he goes to Lowick Church in the hope of seeing Dorothea. Rosamond is technically accomplished, Dorothea full-hearted and emotional in response. Once George Eliot is guilty of an anachronism (chapter 15), mentioning Offenbach's first opera which was not in fact published until 1833, after the time-span of *Middlemarch* closes. It is a rare error.

Authenticity is also conveyed through a number of contemporary allusions, some of which have already been referred to in Chapter 3 of this commentary. Lydgate's need for bodies to dissect leads to a mordant mention of Burke and Hare, the celebrated body-snatchers, murderers of the 1820s. Jacques Lafitte (1767-1844), one of the leaders of the French revolution of 1830, is quoted by Mr Brooke in chapter 38, while the death of the government minister Huskisson (15 September 1830) is jocularly referred to by Raffles in chapter 41. There is, however, a deeper authenticity, the spectrum of biblical reference which supports the moral base of *Middlemarch*. The Bible is the greatest collection of moral and spiritual laws and illustrations of life in our literature. After mottoes from Ecclesiasticus (chapter 69) and Tobias (chapter 74) and passing references in the text throughout, the novel, as it nears its close, has reinforcement in two mottoes from Bunyan, both from *The Pilgrim's Progress* (chapters 79 and 85) which stress the overall moral concern. George Eliot is not Christian by conviction, but her religion of humanity is Christian in practice. Her knowledge of the Bible, like her knowledge of literature, art, science, contemporary affairs and such special areas as medicine, show us the depth, richness and complexity of *Middlemarch*.

The author's voice

Chapter 2 of this commentary contains a number of instances of George Eliot's use of her own voice – or at least the voice of the narrator – in moral comment on character, situation, or in historical, medical, basically factual background or foreground for her fiction. The symbol of the pier-glass referred to earlier is an authorial device for establishing perspective. The reader must be aware of the convention in nineteenth-century fiction, and earlier, which allows the teller to enter her tale as and when she wishes. In *Adam Bede* the author deliberately halts the narrative for one whole chapter in order to explain character and situation. As her narrative art develops, however, we find the author becoming less obtrusive; like Dickens, she learned the art of reticence, letting the narrative flow into climax and crisis without the gloss of authorial directive or rhetoric. But in *Middlemarch* the Prelude and the Finale establish the author's perspective and are unashamedly in her voice. They almost, but not quite, distance us from the fictional experience to come and from that which is over. Structurally they enclose; they are timely reminders that we are reading fiction not living life. Here I intend to give one instance of the author's voice acting as comment and perspective; interestingly, it establishes her as historian of fictional lives in relation to much wider history:

> A great historian, as he insisted on calling himself, who had the happiness to be dead a hundred and twenty years ago, and so to take his place among the colossi whose huge legs our living pettiness is observed to walk under, glories in his copious remarks and digressions as the least imitable part of his work, and especially in those initial chapters to the successive books of his history, where he seems to bring his arm-chair to the proscenium and chat with us in all the lusty ease of his fine English. But Fielding lived when the

days were longer (for time, like money, is measured by our needs), when summer afternoons were spacious, and the clock ticked slowly in the winter evenings. We belated historians must not linger after his example . . . (chapter 15).

The reference is to Henry Fielding in *Tom Jones* (1749), but the content and the tone mark the intellectual narrative maturity of George Eliot. Despite her admiration for Fielding – and there is a warm identification with his confiding intimacy with his readers – we are aware that she is renouncing self-indulgence for narrative directness. This passage serves as 'prelude' to the history of Lydgate but, occurring thus early in the novel, serves to define George Eliot's high awareness of her art. Thereafter the authorial commentary is part of the total relevance – nothing is extraneous to the design in terms of character, situation, image, symbol, factual background or fictional foreground. We are aware of the author's character in her fiction, but not, I think, obtrusively aware as we are of Thackeray's in *Vanity Fair*. What we are aware of, and this insistently but still not obtrusively, are the standards of morality and conduct, responsibility and pride in work, honesty, integrity, altruistic endeavour, dedication, which she would have us observe and respect as codes of living.

5 SPECIMEN PASSAGE
AND
COMMENTARY

5.1 SPECIMEN PASSAGE

She locked herself in her room. She needed time to get used to her maimed consciousness, her poor lopped life, before she could walk steadily to the place allotted her. A new searching light had fallen on her husband's character and she could not judge him leniently: the twenty years in which she had believed in him and venerated him by virtue of his concealments came back with particulars that made them seem an odious deceit. He had married her with that bad past life hidden behind him and she had no faith left to protest his innocence of the worst that was imputed to him. Her honest ostentatious nature made the sharing of a merited dishonour as bitter as it could be to any mortal.

But this imperfectly-taught woman, whose phrases and habits were an odd patchwork, had a loyal spirit within her. The man whose prosperity she had shared through nearly half a life, and who had unvaryingly cherished her – now that punishment had befallen him, it was not possible to her in any sense to forsake him. There is a forsaking which still sits at the same board and lies on the same couch with the forsaken soul, withering it the more by unloving proximity. She knew, when she locked her door, that she should unlock ir ready to go down to her unhappy husband and espouse his sorrow, and say of his guilt, I will mourn and not reproach. But she needed time to gather up her strength; she needed to sob out her farewell to all the gladness and pride of her life. When she had resolved to go down, she prepared herself by some little acts which might seem mere folly to a hard onlooker; they were her way of expressing to all spectators visible or invisible that she had begun a new life in which she embraced humiliation. She took off all her ornaments and put on a plain black gown, and instead of wearing her much-adorned cap and large bows of hair, she brushed her hair down and put on a plain bonnet-cap, which made her look suddenly like an early Methodist.

Bulstrode, who knew that his wife had been out and had come in saying that she was not well, had spent the time in an agitation equal to hers. He had looked forward to her learning the truth from others, and had acquiesced in that probability, as something easier to him than any confession. But now that he imagined the moment of her knowledge come, he awaited the result in anguish. His daughters had been obliged to consent to leave him, and though he had allowed some food to be brought to him, he had not touched it. He felt himself perishing slowly in unpitied misery. Perhaps he should never see his wife's face with affection in it again. And if he turned to God there seemed to be no answer but the pressure of retribution.

It was eight o'clock in the evening before the door opened and his wife entered. He dared not look up at her. He sat with his eyes bent down, and as she went towards him she thought he looked smaller – he seemed so withered and shrunken. A movement of new compassion and old tenderness went through her like a great wave, and putting one hand on his which rested on the arm of the chair, she said, solemnly but kindly –

'Look up, Nicholas.'

He raised his eyes with a little start and looked at her half-amazed for a moment: her pale face, her changed, mourning dress, the trembling about her mouth, all said, 'I know'; and her hands and eyes rested gently on him. He burst out crying and they cried together, she sitting at his side. They could not yet speak to each other of the shame which she was bearing with him, or of the acts which had brought it down on them. His confession was silent, and her promise of faithfulness was silent. Open-minded as she was, she nevertheless shrank from the words which would have expressed their mutual consciousness, as she would have shrunk from flakes of fire. She could not say' 'How much is only slander and false suspicion?' and he did not say, 'I am innocent.'   (chapter 74).

5.2 COMMENTARY

This is one of the finest pieces of direct writing in *Middlemarch*, with commentary, investigation of consciousness and reaction all forming part of this complete insight into Harriet Bulstrode in crisis. The use of the word 'locked' in the first sentence carries a peculiar force; Harriet is symbolically locking herself away from the world in order to think, but she – and Bulstrode – are already locked in the prison of the past, the present and the future because of the revelations and suspicions. Linking imagery is used like 'lopped' and 'maimed', both physical terms which here convey mental and emotional suffering, the idea of injury which is permanent, the first associated with trees and the lopping of branches, integral to them; the second with wounding, again perhaps permanent. The word 'allotted' has the force of 'prescribed', and is therefore connected with the 'prison' of the future. 'A searching light' is effective, since it contrasts with the 'moral lantern' that Bulstrode himself has been wont to turn on people, while 'by virtue of his concealments' is fine irony, since his secrets are vices not virtues in any sense. Note the effective use of simple words like 'bad' and 'worst' – the simple and honest words which Harriet herself would use – to convey the obloquy of Bulstrode's conduct, and note also the last sentence of the paragraph which leaves the reader in doubt as to how she will react and thus moves us towards the tension of decision.

George Eliot herself has no doubts about Harriet. Words like 'imperfectly-taught' and 'patchwork' are offset by 'loyal spirit', which in fact is the moral index to Harriet's love. And this is real love, seen in contrast to the egoistic 'patchwork' of Rosamond's love for Lydgate and Casaubon's for Dorothea – and we think how 'perfectly-taught' by contrast those two have been; 'patchwork' also underlines the simple domesticity of Harriet's domestic habits. Her generosity of spirit is further emphasised by the contrast, for 'unloving proximity', impossible for Harriet, defines the reactions of Rosamond and Casaubon to their respective partners as they reach adversity. This whole scene is important in the moral structure of the novel. His 'cherished' balances her 'venerated' in the first paragraph; 'twenty years' balances the 'half a life' in the second. Both are redolent of loyalty and love. The word 'withering' in this long second paragraph anticipates the 'withered' appearance of her husband in paragraph 4, and it is true to say that both their lives are withered by what has happened.

Notice also the word 'forsake' and its derivatives, the repetition of which is a considered stress on hardness *and* at the same time calls to mind the fact that Bulstrode at this very time considers himself forsaken. The unlocking of the door is factual and symbolic, indicating her choosing to embrace giving rather than indulging in rejection or self-pity. The use of the word 'espouse' is particularly fine, since in a sense she is marrying again – making her vows again – to this guilty husband; yet in the same sentence the use of 'mourn' conveys her sadness at the death of their past pure (in her eyes and practice) marriage. Harriet's use of the internal monologue asserts her decision; it contrasts effectively with the two unanswered questions – both in the form of a monologue – with which the passage here closes.

Harriet's change of clothing and her putting on of the bonnet-cap symbolise her acceptance of humiliation; they do more than that, for they are at once mourning for the past and the reordered life of the present. Again there is a structural link here, for Dorothea chooses a new dress when she faces the crisis of her life over Will and Rosamond, while her removal of her widow's cap in fact signals her new life *and* (although she does not realise it at the time) the possibility of marriage to Will.

The switch to Bulstrode in paragraph 3 is dramatically and humanly effective; the first few lines show that even in this crisis Bulstrode has behaved consistently, for just as he would have others tell his wife of his delinquencies, so he has Mrs Abel administer the liquor to Raffles. He is, so to speak, always at one remove from the commitment of personal action. The shorter paragraph has the dramatic immediacy of focusing on complete isolation, for Bulstrode, who has set so much store by prayer in the past, realises that it is useless now. His situation is beyond prayer. Notice that the sentences get shorter, then a little longer again, almost as if they are the index to Bulstrode's emotional temperature, fluctuating with anxiety, as he waits.

The fourth and final paragraph is redolent with dramatic tension – and a kind of narrative dramatic irony – for although we know what Harriet intends to do, Bulstrode doesn't. We have already commented on 'withered', but we should also consider 'shrunken' and 'smaller', for George Eliot is trying to represent visually what has actually happened – Bulstrode is diminished in moral and Christian stature and this appears consonant with his physical appearance. Yet it is true that after a great shock or suffering people do seem to be smaller. There is a wonderful blending of the past and the present in Harriet's 'new compassion' and 'old tenderness', symbolic of the new life having to subsume the past one, while the 'wave' (and water gives life in *Middlemarch*) can either submerge or hold up. As the image is of Harriet, we have no doubt that she will sustain her husband, and her first words endorse this. 'Look up' implies 'Carry your head high', i.e. be brave enough to face life, with the unvoiced qualification that she (Harriet) will support her husband. Looks are used to convey what he hopes, that she does indeed know and is unchanged towards him. The only spoken words are the three we have mentioned, but here silence is more effective than words in conveying the mutuality of their suffering, and poignantly the mutuality of their love and dependence. The use of the word 'gently' almost carries the force of her forgiveness *and* her blessing of her husband, while the tears are more eloquent than words. There is a strong implication that there is a time for words and a time for silence, and that words in fact might have undermined Harriet's profession of faithfulness.

A compassionate irony embraces the idea of complete trust, ennobling Harriet and also Bulstrode, not merely in her shadow, but positively because he had gone beyond the point where he can tell his wife lies, his whole life with her in a sense having been one. In this last paragraph the word 'shrunken' used of Bulstrode is taken up and applied to Harriet, being twice repeated as 'shrank' and 'shrunk' to indicate her fear of words which would incriminate her husband, the 'flakes of fire' conveying the hell it would be to her to hear them. This curious triplication, as in the derivatives of 'forsake', has the effect of emphasis, extreme suffering through repetition. I suggest that it shows George Eliot's attention to structural awareness in the part as well as the whole, that there is an aesthetic verbal patterning which is part of the artistic and emotional coherence – or structure – of *Middlemarch*.

Moral crises are the pivots on which George Eliot's novels turn. In contradistinction to her niece, Harriet responds to adversity with love, faith, practicality and, above all, the human sympathy so needed by her husband. Her decision represents rightness of conduct, and it is paralleled on a number of levels in *Middlemarch*. Think of Casaubon's kind words to Dorothea as she sits up waiting for him as he temporarily escapes from the small shivering centre of self; think of Rosamond's telling Dorothea that Will loves her, Dorothea, as she too temporarily forsakes the image of propriety which she and others consider her to be. Think of Mary's loyalty to Fred over the years of his irresponsibility, or of Fred's loyalty to her despite his acknowledged shortcomings. Think of Dorothea's generous belief in Lydgate's innocence and of her unselfconscious expression of it to that emotionally beleaguered man; think of Farebrother's renunciation of Mary and of his sympathy, understanding and insight which bring out the best in Fred on Mary's behalf.

These movements of humanity and compassion represent George Eliot's belief in practical and sympathetic altruism, and in this way the passage above is typical. It is enhanced, as I have said, not only through the images and repetitions, but also as much by what is *not* said. Commentary and silence blend in the consciousness of character and, as always, the psychological consistency with which George Eliot presents and sustains character is exemplary.

6 CRITICAL RECEPTION

6.1 CONTEMPORARY AND NINETEENTH-CENTURY VIEWS

Middlemarch was recognised as a distinguished novel by contemporary reviewers, but there were some who still considered that the earlier novels were superior. *Adam Bede* was a particular favourite, the reviewer in *The Times* and the much longer notice in the *Quarterly Review* agreeing that *Middlemarch* was inferior in the 'liveliness, variety and picturesquness of its great predecessor'. The first reviewers, of course, considered the novel as a serial, and were in fact writing about the effect – and sometimes the completeness – of each part as it came out. Reviewers in the *Athenaeum* and the *Spectator* considered that although it appeared as a serial, *Middlemarch* was in fact completed before it began to be published. As we have seen from Section 1.4 of this commentary this was not true, for Book VIII was not completed until the second week in September 1872, before the last three books of the novel were published.

There was some criticism of the ending of Book I from the *Examiner*, which took the view that not enough expectation was aroused before the next instalment. The *Edinburgh* reviewer saw the serial issue as holding out the hope that 'the real hero and the real heroine' would be brought together ultimately. Since this undoubtedly means Dorothea and Lydgate, one sees that serial publication provided 'Possibilities' which hardly exist for the twentieth-century reader who has the whole novel before him. One reviewer could not distinguish whether Ladislaw or Lydgate would ultimately secure Dorothea, which suggests highly subjective and careless reading on his part.

The Prelude provided some difficulty for many reviewers, since it appeared to indicate that the central focus of the novel was to be Dorothea. Even Henry James, admittedly without the hindsight that we possess, felt that George Eliot had been drawn away into her 'Study of Provincial Life' from the concerns of her central character, not realising that it was her intention to draw that central character into the concerns of Rosamond and Lydgate as well as Farebrother and obliquely into those of Bulstrode, her sister and Sir James. As W. J. Harvey rightly notes (see Further

Reading), the reviewer in the *Academy* came close to the major subject of the novel when he observed that 'its incidents are taken from the inner life, as the action is developed by the direct influence of mind on mind and character on character', the 'material circumstances of the outer world' providing 'a background of perfect realistic truth to a profoundly imaginative psychological study'. Some critics considered that *Middlemarch* dealt with the 'woman' question and that it was in essence an attack on 'modern society' for imposing crippling conditions especially on women 'of high ideal enthusiasm'.

Just as the Prelude had caused a certain degree of disquiet, so the Finale led to accusations of some misrepresentations on George Eliot's part in the first edition of *Middlemarch*, where the 'prosaic conditions' of Dorothea's life in the 'neighbourhood of Middlemarch' are blamed for her subsequently muted idealism. The *British Quarterly Review, Spectator,* the *Athenaeum* and *The Times* all pointed out the inconsistency, and it is interesting to note that for the single volume edition of 1874 the George Eliot revised and heavily cut what she had originally written. Dorothea's 'prosaic conditions' are altered to 'amidst the conditions of an imperfect social state'. As Jerome Beaty (see Further Reading) has pointed out, the final version is much more generalised than the first, which had castigated the limitations in the education of women and society for supporting 'rules of conduct which are in flat contradiction with its own loudly-asserted beliefs'. George Eliot, ever sensitive to those reviews which Lewes permitted her to see, obviously toned down what she had originally written as being either too strong or not even quite true of the young, deluded Dorothea.

On one area contemporary and modern criticism are in some agreement; it is summarised in *The Times* reviewer's assertion that there is a 'mean and commonplace effect' about the unravelling of Bulstrode's and Ladislaw's past, stressing what seems to be one of the novel's weaknesses, though Bulstrode as a character was regarded as a triumph by many of the contemporary reviewers. In fact much of the critical appraisal was given over, inevitably at that time, to descriptive praise of character presentation. Mrs Cadwallader, Mr Brooke and the Garths came in for much appreciation, and sometimes there was an attempt to link character and structure, as in the *London Quarterly Review*'s analysis of Bulstrode.

The omniscient author also attracted some comment, the *Edinburgh Review* considering that George Eliot as 'Chorus is too continually present' while the *Spectator* said (of her characters) that 'George Eliot has favourites and aversions, and deals hardly with the latter'. Rosamond is an instance of the latter, and, obviously, Ladislaw of the former. But even here there is some subtlety, as a few reviewers see Dorothea's coming together with Ladislaw as a further muting of her idealism since he is manifestly not morally good enough for her anyway. Moreover, *Middlemarch* is generally regarded as a pessimistic novel by contemporary reviewers.

Henry James stands out among these reviewers because of his 'conception of aesthetic unity', but as the century draws on after George Eliot's death in 1880 there is little criticism of note on *Middlemarch*. In his essay 'George Eliot as Author' reprinted in his *Modern Guides of English Thought in Matters of Faith* (1888) Richard Holt Hutton treats *Middlemarch* in some depth, for although he finds it 'profoundly melancholy' he proceeds to analyse the character of Dorothea, observing that George Eliot has Dorothea marry twice, and that neither marriage is ideal, 'though the second is an improvement on the first'. He picks out the humour and Mr Brooke in particular for praise. Oscar Browning, in his *Life of George Eliot* (1890) has a chapter on *Middlemarch* and George Eliot's following works with hardly a critical glance. An earlier writer, Mathilde Blind, produced a monograph on *George Eliot* in the 'Eminent Women Series' (1883) which contains some fine analyses of Dorothea and Casaubon. She asserts that 'there is a distinct indication of her [George Eliot's] attitude towards the aspirations and clearly formulated demands of the women of the 19th century'.

6.2 TWENTIETH-CENTURY CRITICISM

The writer and critic, Leslie Stephen, devalues *Middlemarch* in his 'English Men of Letters' book on *George Eliot* (Macmillan, 1902), observing that it 'lacks the peculiar charm of the early work' and accuses the author of adopting a 'position of philosophical detachment which somehow exhibits her characters in rather a distorting light'. It is a strange and wayward judgement. Early twentieth-century criticism of *Middlemarch* is undistinguished. I intend here to concentrate on the work of two modern critics who examine and establish the nature of George Eliot's art.

F. R. Leavis in *The Great Tradition* (Chatto & Windus 1948) argues unequivocally that only 'one book can, as a whole (though not without qualification), be said to represent her genius. That, of course, is *Middlemarch*.' He goes on to enumerate the main aspects of its greatness – the range and 'real knowledge' of the various classes and how they live, together with 'a profound analysis of the individual'. The intellectual appraisal of 'an intellectual *manqué*, (Casaubon) he notes as typical of George Eliot's achievement in *Middlemarch* (obviously the same is true of her presentation of Lydgate). In addition there is the pathos of Casaubon's situation, 'the critical quality of George Eliot's irony', and her nobility. This he applies to the treatment of Casaubon and to Lydgate, 'of whom pre-eminently it can be said that he could have been done only by someone who knew the intellectual life from the inside . . .'. George Eliot is able to make his 'intellectual passion' 'concrete'. Leavis finds a 'poetic justice' in Lydgate's succumbing to the 'simple ego' of Rosamond, and tellingly notes that some of the exchanges between women – witness Mary Garth and Rosamond – 'give us some of George Eliot's finest comedy'. He also greatly praises the presentation of Bulstrode ('George Eliot knows from the inside') with its freedom from satire, but with an analysis 'that only an intelligence lighted by compassion can attain'. And then, as if stating the obvious, Leavis asserts that the weakness of the book 'is in Dorothea'. He sums up Dorothea and Will with commendable economy:

> George Eliot's valuation of Will Ladislaw, in short, is Dorothea's, just as Will's of Dorothea is George Eliot's. Dorothea, to put it another way, is a product of George Eliot's own 'soul-hunger' – another day-dream ideal self.

This failure, says Leavis, is one of creative vitality.

Professor Hardy's *The Novels of George Eliot: a study in form* (Athlone Press, 1959) ranges over all of George Eliot's novels and shows what a self-conscious artist she was. Mrs Hardy sets out to establish that 'the apparently rambling and circumstantial expression of her spirit has its own formal principles'. In *Middlemarch* she demonstrates that some changes were made 'to meet the practical problems of serial form, but they show her interest in the unity of the novel as a whole', for example the movement away from Dorothea to the Middlemarch spectrum before the end of the first part. She further shows how George Eliot's 'organization, like Shakespeare's, extends, for instance, to her imagery', and of course to her characters. She tells us that George Eliot exposes Dorothea's lack of education (and Rosamond's), and later investigates the structural importance of the contrasted pair in George Eliot's fiction, though the 'classifying division into egoist and altruist is varied from novel to novel'. She notices the Book titles and their unifying relevance ('Waiting for Death' and 'The Dead Hand') and later, in the brilliant chapter called 'Possibilities' notes the tendency of nineteenth- (and perhaps twentieth-) century readers to see or hope for a coming together of Dorothea and Lydgate.

Mrs Hardy analyses the nature of the author's use of her own voice whether intimate, prophetic or dramatic, and all three are employed in *Middlemarch*. In the first George Eliot often moves from the particular example to the general statement. The prophetic voice is largely in abeyance in *Middlemarch*, but the dramatic voice, and here Mrs Hardy concentrates on the presentation of Bulstrode, is an effective commentary on his consciousness. It is even more subtle than that, for just when we are expecting George Eliot to continue her commentary, she withdraws. As Mrs Hardy says, 'The voice is as expressive in its absence as in its presence'. It is a subtle piece of criticism, typical of the book as a whole. Mrs Hardy also discusses the 'Scene as Image' (the disenchantment of Dorothea's boudoir in *Middlemarch*) and 'The Ironical Image'. In *Middlemarch* there are 'three important repeated images, the image of the water, the image of the dark or narrow place, and the image of the mirror'. For the student of *Middlemarch* this section is essential reading, for it shows how varied and wide-ranging George Eliot's formal subtlety is.

REVISION QUESTIONS

1. Show how the story of Dorothea is woven into the other main narratives of *Middlemarch*.

2. To what extent does George Eliot succeed in preserving a strict neutrality in her presentation of Dorothea and Casaubon?

3. How far is *Middlemarch* a novel which deals with 'failed idealism'?

4. 'A treasure-house of detail, but an indifferent whole.' Say how far you would agree or disagree with this estimate by Henry James of *Middlemarch*.

5. In what ways is Lydgate a weak character? You should refer closely to the text in your answer *or* 'An unsympathetic study in egoism'. Write an essay saying whether you agree or disagree with this comment on George Eliot's presentation of Rosamond.

6. In what ways are the Garths the moral 'centre' of *Middlemarch*.

7. Write an essay on George Eliot's use of *either* imagery *or* symbolism in *Middlemarch*.

8. Write an essay on any character not mentioned above, showing how George Eliot succeeds in achieving psychological consistency in his/her presentation.

9. How far is the background of (a) political and (b) medical reform necessary to our understanding of George Eliot's intentions in *Middlemarch*?

10. Write an appreciation of any aspect of *Middlemarch* which interests you and which has not been mentioned in the foregoing questions.

FURTHER READING

Texts

Two annotated texts are currently available. These are: *Middlemarch*, ed. W. J. Harvey (Penguin English Library (Harmondsworth, Middx., 1965)), and *Middlemarch*, ed. Bert G. Hornback (Norton Critical Editions) (New York: Norton, 1977).

Biography

The definitive biography is by Gordon S. Haight. It is simply called: *George Eliot: a biography* (Oxford: Clarendon Press, 1968; Paperback 1981). Of the other biographies only Ruby Redinger's *George Eliot: the emergent self* (London: Heinemann, 1975) is of positive value, and this depends heavily on psychological interpretation.

Letters

J. W. Cross's *George Eliot's Life as Related in Her Letters* (1885) has been entirely superseded by Gordon Haight's *The George Eliot Letters*, 9 vols (London: Yale, 1954–78), which includes letters to and from George Eliot and G. H. Lewes as well as extracts from their diaries and journals.

Scholarly investigations

Anna Theresa Kitchel's *Quarry for Middlemarch* (Berkeley: University of California Press, 1950) contains a number of interesting notes on medicine, dates, motives and scenes for *Middlemarch*. Jerome Beaty's *Middlemarch from Notebook to Novel* (Urbana, Illinois: University of Illinois Press, 1960) examines the fusion of the 'Miss Brooke' and Middlemarch elements of the novel and evidence of rewriting in the manuscript, while there is a particularly rich and stimulating focus on chapter 81, where Dorothea visits Rosamond for the second time.

Criticism

Contemporary reception has been referred to in chapter 6, but of the nineteenth-century critics whose work is still available and important, the student is directed to Henry James's review of *Middlemarch*, reprinted in his *The House of Fiction*, ed. Leon Edel (London: Hart-Davis, 1957). George Eliot's reputation suffered a decline until the 1940s, when two books, Joan Bennett's *George Eliot: her mind and her art* (Cambridge University Press, 1948) and F. R. Leavis's *The Great Tradition* (London: Chatto & Windus) were published in the same year. Mrs Bennett treats *Middlemarch* (pp. 160–80) as 'George Eliot's supreme achievement'. F. R. Leavis has been discussed in Chapter 6. As early as 1925 Virginia Woolf had asserted (in *The Common Reader, First Series*):

> It is not that her power diminishes, for, to our thinking, it is at its highest in the mature *Middlemarch*, the magnificent book which with all its imperfections is one of the few English novels written for grown-up people.

Barbara Hardy in *The Novels of George Eliot: a study in form* (London: Athlone Press, 1959) established beyond doubt George Eliot's greatness as a formal artist, as we have seen in Chapter 6 of this study. Mrs Hardy's later collection of essays on George Eliot, *Particularities: readings in George Eliot* (London: Peter Owen, 1982) contains four essays on *Middlemarch*, two of which examine closely two of the important chapters in the novel. Mrs Hardy edited a stimulating collection of essays in *Middlemarch: critical approaches to the novel* (London: Athlone Press, 1967), which covers a wide range of critical investigation, with studies of Dorothea, Lydgate and Casaubon, imagery, structure, and contemporary reception. Other interesting critical studies are W. J. Harvey's *The Art of George Eliot* (London: Chatto & Windus, 1961) and the collection of essays in *This Particular Web*, ed. Ian Adam (Toronto: University of Toronto Press, 1975). The influence of Darwin and evolutionary theory is brilliantly charted in Gillian Beer's *Darwin's Plots* (London: Routledge & Kegan Paul, 1983; *Middlemarch* pp. 149–80). A good general introduction to George Eliot is to be found in Rosemary Ashton's *George Eliot* (Oxford University Press, 1983, 'Past Masters' Series).

MACMILLAN STUDENTS' NOVELS

General Editor: JAMES GIBSON

The Macmillan Students' Novels are low-priced, new editions of major classics, aimed at the first examination candidate. Each volume contains:

* enough explanation and background material to make the novels accessible — and rewarding — to pupils with little or no previous knowledge of the author or the literary period;

* detailed notes elucidate matters of vocabulary, interpretation and historical background;

* eight pages of plates comprising facsimiles of manuscripts and early editions, portraits of the author and photographs of the geographical setting of the novels.

MILTON: PARADISE LOST
A. E. Dyson and Julian Lovelock

POETRY OF THE FIRST WORLD
WAR
Dominic Hibberd

ALEXANDER POPE: THE RAPE OF
THE LOCK
John Dixon Hunt

SHELLEY: SHORTER POEMS &
LYRICS
Patrick Swinden

SPENSER: THE FAERIE QUEEN
Peter Bayley

TENNYSON: IN MEMORIAM
John Dixon Hunt

THIRTIES POETS: 'THE AUDEN
GROUP'
Ronald Carter

WORDSWORTH: LYRICAL
BALLADS
A. R. Jones and W. Tydeman

WORDSWORTH: THE PRELUDE
W. J. Harvey and R. Gravil

W. B. YEATS: POEMS 1919–1935
E. Cullingford

W. B. YEATS: LAST POEMS
Jon Stallworthy

THE NOVEL AND PROSE

JANE AUSTEN: EMMA
David Lodge

JANE AUSTEN: NORTHANGER
ABBEY AND PERSUASION
B. C. Southam

JANE AUSTEN: SENSE AND
SENSIBILITY, PRIDE AND
PREJUDICE AND MANSFIELD
PARK
B. C. Southam

CHARLOTTE BRONTË: JANE EYRE
AND VILLETTE
Miriam Allott

EMILY BRONTË: WUTHERING
HEIGHTS
Miriam Allott

BUNYAN: THE PILGRIM'S
PROGRESS
R. Sharrock

CONRAD: HEART OF DARKNESS,
NOSTROMO AND UNDER
WESTERN EYES
C. B. Cox

CONRAD: THE SECRET AGENT
Ian Watt

CHARLES DICKENS: BLEAK
HOUSE
A. E. Dyson

CHARLES DICKENS: DOMBEY
AND SON AND LITTLE DORRITT
Alan Shelston

CHARLES DICKENS: HARD TIMES,
GREAT EXPECTATIONS AND OUR
MUTUAL FRIEND
N. Page

GEORGE ELIOT: MIDDLEMARCH
Patrick Swinden

GEORGE ELIOT: THE MILL ON
THE FLOSS AND SILAS MARNER
R. P. Draper

HENRY FIELDING: TOM JONES
Neil Compton

E. M. FORSTER: A PASSAGE TO
INDIA
Malcolm Bradbury

HARDY: THE TRAGIC NOVELS
R. P. Draper

HENRY JAMES: WASHINGTON
SQUARE AND THE PORTRAIT OF
A LADY
Alan Shelston

JAMES JOYCE: DUBLINERS AND A
PORTRAIT OF THE ARTIST AS A
YOUNG MAN
Morris Beja

D. H. LAWRENCE: THE RAINBOW
AND WOMEN IN LOVE
Colin Clarke

D. H. LAWRENCE: SONS AND
LOVERS
Gamini Salgado

SWIFT: GULLIVER'S TRAVELS
Richard Gravil